HOW TO HIRE LAWYERS

A Guide to Hiring the Best Attorney
for Your Legal Issue

www.HowToHireLawyers.com

Copyright © 2017 José M. Bautista, Andrew S. LeRoy, Anthony S. McDaniel, Michael Rapp, Molly M. Hastings, Frederick W. Bryant, Thomas P. Bryant, Zachary Goff, Jennifer Oswald Brown, Isaac D. Keppler, Jeffrey L. Wagoner and Carrie Mulholland Brous.

First Edition
All rights reserved.

No part of this publication may be reproduced, stored in a retrieval system or transmitted in any form or by any means, electronic, mechanical, photocopying, recording, scanning or otherwise, except under the terms of the Copyright, Designs and Patents Act 1988 or under the terms of a license issued by the Copyright Licensing Agency Ltd.

Legal Disclaimer

The publisher and the authors make no representations or warranties with respect to the accuracy or completeness of the contents of this work and specifically disclaim all warranties, including without limitation warranties for a particular purpose. No warranty may be created or extended by sales or promotional materials. The advice and strategies contained herein may not be suitable for every situation.

Neither the publisher nor the authors shall be liable for damages arising herefrom. The fact that an organization or website is referred to in this work as a citation and/or a potential source of further information does not mean that the author or the publisher endorses the information the organization or website may provide or recommendations it may make.

Further, readers should be aware that Internet websites or web pages listed in this work may have changed or disappeared between when this work was written and when it is read.

www.HowToHireLawyers.com

Contents

Foreword vii

Accolades ix

Chapter 1: Fraud Attorneys
By Carrie Mulholland Brous 1

Chapter 2: Family Attorneys
By Jennifer Oswald Brown, Member, and Erin Mayfield Craig,
Domestic Attorney 11

Chapter 3: Workers' Compensation Attorneys
By Fred Bryant and Tom Bryant 23

Chapter 4: Employment Attorneys
By Isaac D. Keppler 39

Chapter 5: Taxation Attorneys
By Zachary Goff 47

Chapter 6: Criminal Law Attorneys
By Molly Hastings 59

Chapter 7: Bankruptcy Attorneys
By Jeffrey L. Wagoner 69

Chapter 8: Insurance Dispute Attorneys
By José M. Bautista 87

Chapter 9: Auto Accident Attorneys
By Anthony S. McDaniel 99

Chapter 10: Nursing Home Neglect Attorneys
By Andrew LeRoy 115

Chapter 11: Consumer Attorneys
By Michael Rapp 127

Acknowledgements 139

Foreword

Andrew and I cut our teeth as lawyers for marquee plaintiff's law firms in Kansas City. Co-counseling on complex cases against corporations such as Teledyne Motors, Cabela's, and Farmer's Insurance, we got to know each other and learned that our professional styles were complimentary. More importantly, we learned of our shared passion for helping people who couldn't help themselves. Our partnership naturally formed and we've been suing corporations and their insurance companies for our clients ever since.

Over the years, people called the office and inquired about criminal charges, tax planning, divorces, etc. They continued their inquiries to our firm even after we explained that we specialize in plaintiff's injury litigation. We were not always certain these consumers visited the lawyers that we referred. Sometimes, they simply gave up. We realized that people needed an introduction to the various legal specialties.

So, we put together established Kansas City lawyers who excelled in their respective fields and demonstrated a social conscience not only in their work but also their lives. Each practitioner generously agreed to take time from his or her busy practice to author a chapter geared toward non-lawyers. The product was this book.

Note that our laws are based on a system of precedent, which means they are constantly changing, and some of citations in the book may be outdated by time of publication. Also understand that although this book is not meant to be an advertisement, it may have that effect and the choice of an attorney is an important decision that should not be based on advertisements alone. It is also not meant to be legal advice, as every case needs to be judged on its own merits and the references in the book may not apply to a particular set of facts or legal circumstances. Our goal for this book was just to reduce some of the mystery and apprehension about approaching law firms and to guide consumers to lawyers that best fit their situation.

Nothing can really replace a meeting with your potential attorney. Andrew and I make it a rule to meet all our new clients in person, and we recommend that you do the same before selecting your attorney.

- José Bautista & Andrew LeRoy

Accolades

"Where was this book when I started practicing? A tremendous resource if you are new to practice or just new to that area of law. It's great to see KCMBA members collaborating on this project. This book will be helpful to anyone looking for a lawyer on a variety of legal topics. Working together, they've covered a lot of legal ground, an outstanding collaboration!"

Kelly McCambridge – KCMBA Membership Co-Chair
McCambridge Law LLC
1308 NE Windsor Drive
Lee's Summit, MO 64086
Kelly@mccambridgelaw.com
816.389.8345

"It's about time that someone published a basic guide that Kansas City consumers can understand. I'm proud to see that one of our members put it together. Thank you Jose, Andrew, and the lawyers at Bautista LeRoy."

Carlos Gomez,
President of the Hispanic Chamber of Commerce
of Greater Kansas City

"Choosing an attorney with confidence is a difficult process for many individuals. This book is an excellent primer on the basic tenants on what type of lawyer an individual might need, what qualities to look for in a reputable attorney, and what the client can do to prepare for the business relationship with that attorney. The authors represented in this book are all experienced and reputable in his or her respective fields. Combined, they have thousands of hours of experience with clients and cases. This would be a fantastic resource for every law practitioner to have on hand, both to educate potential clients on some of the actions the client can take to make the transaction with his or her attorney run smoothly, and to serve as a resource for the practitioner for areas of law that he or she may not be as familiar with."

Danielle A. Merrick, J.D., LL.M.
Associate Staff Director
UMKC School of Law
Entrepreneurial Legal Services Clinic

CHAPTER 1:
Fraud Attorneys

By: Carrie Mulholland Brous

"We live in an era of fraud in America. [But] fraud and short- sighted thinking have never, ever worked. Not once. Eventually you get caught, things go south."

Mark Baum, *The Big Short*

I. Introduction

When you think of American corporate culture, fraud does not immediately come to mind. Instead, we think of free markets, entrepreneurs and capitalism. As Americans, we are taught from a young age that with a good idea and elbow grease, anyone can make something good into something great. While this framework of positivity and possibility is  the bedrock of our American experience, often there is a silent cost to our corporate culture – corruption.

In the moment, it's more comfortable to see corruption as something that happens other places but not here. And yet, the reality is that fraud is everywhere. Banking, investments, pharmaceuticals, skilled nursing, hospitals, government contractors and publically traded giants are all tainted by fraud.

With the possibility of two distinct choices there always exists the possibility of things heading south, but what tips the scales in favor of fraud when a more noble action exists? The answer is straightforward: greed. In a culture of capitalism and competition, cheating becomes a likely by-product.

If you ask what the purpose of a company is, most people will say a company exists to make money – money for owners, executives, employees, and shareholders. In America, we value money and oftentimes equate it with success. Companies make money by tending to the bottom line and rewarding the performance of those who keep the numbers running in the right direction.

Inherent in this is the possibility of companies incenting fraud. The theory goes, the more you bend the rules and get into the blurred areas of gray, the more you and everyone around you has the potential for greater financial reward.

Bending the rules into illegal territories can take many forms. For example, any publically traded company must abide by generally accepted accounting rules And yet, the action of bending the rules and accounting for things in a different way, even just slightly different, can create higher earnings, rising stock prices, and an everyone-wins mentality as participants make more money.

For example, pharmaceutical sales representatives are not supposed to sell drugs for things not approved by the FDA. Yet, there is so much more to sell (and money to make and stock prices to inflate) with flexible label boundaries and opportunities to sell beyond those boundaries. Quality assurance managers make sure things like drugs and loans meet certain standards, but there's the possibility to make more of what you are selling if quality assurance is marginalized and silenced.

Medicare patients rely on healthcare providers to provide only services they need. But, companies serving these patients can make more money if the Medicare benefit is used to the fullest extent (whether or not it is medically necessary). Likewise, it becomes easier to secure a successful government contract if the bid is sweetened with lunch and a few gifts. After all, what does it really matter if you win the contract and make more money?

II. THE LITTLE FRAUD ADDS UP

The bottom line is a powerful thing, and commerce is beholden to it. Within this power struggle, fraud is always present. This is where whistleblowers come in.

The government recognizes that rewarding whistleblowers who come forward with insider information of fraud is one of the most effective ways to stop corruption. When awarding a $22 million award to a whistleblower who came forward with accounting fraud inside publically traded Monsanto, the head of the SEC whistleblower office, said "[w]ithout this whistleblower's courage, information and assistance, it would have been extremely difficult for law enforcement to discover this securities fraud on its own." *See* August 30, 2016 SEC Press Release (quoting Jane Norberg, Acting Chief of SEC Office of the Whistleblower). The SEC recognizes that company employees are in "unique positions behind-the-scenes to unravel complex or deeply buried wrongdoing." *See id.*

It seems fraud is more prevalent than any of us might have once believed. Today, fraud is fodder for headlines with the now-familiar players Enron, Madoff, Wells Fargo, and Lehman Brothers in the lead roles. As Congress and prosecutors prime themselves to ask those famous fraudsters questions, is it any wonder why the public now views whistleblower stories as the stuff from which books and movies are made?

But I want to be clear – fraud that is worthy of whistleblowing isn't always something that lands on the evening news or in a headline in your news feed. Fraud typically begins on a minor scale, usually small cheats that through several people and over several days adds up significantly over the months and years. It can be little things, like: a cheat on the number of minutes recorded as therapy provided to a Medicare beneficiary or a cheat on accounting for the cost of customer rebates. A small number soon creates a big impact when it scales company-wide to hundreds and thousands of transactions over long periods of time.

III. THE POTENTIAL TO BLOW THE WHISTLE IS EVERYWHERE

Doing business in this country requires playing by the government's rules. Anyone can become a potential defendant, from publically traded companies who don't adhere to accounting principles, to any company receiving federal or state funds, to government contractors paid directly from the government. Think: highly regulated – regulated by the Securities and Exchange Commission (SEC), the Food and Drug Administration (FDA) and the Environmental Protection Agency (EPA).

The director of the SEC enforcement division said whistleblowers have had a *"transformative impact"* since the SEC whistleblowing program was implemented in 2011. *See* August 30, 2016 SEC Press Release (quoting Andrew Ceresney, Director of SEC Division of Enforcement). The possibilities are endless, and the whistleblower can *transform* commerce in America.

Since beefing up the whistleblowing laws in the 1980s to provide more financial incentive for whistleblowers to come forward, *billions* (with a *b*) have been recovered for the government and awarded to whistleblowers as finder's fees.

Whistleblowers are as varied as the fraud they report. They are: company or regional vice presidents, assistants or secretaries to a vice president, mail room clerks, accountants, nurses or physical therapists, or managers in charge of quality control. Whistleblowers aren't always inside the company. They can be a competitor who knows the inside of a government bidding process or a consultant. Anyone with inside information can blow the whistle on fraud.

IV. WHERE DO YOU GO FROM HERE?

If greed is the fuel for fraud, and fraud is everywhere, what do you do when you know about fraud? Two things: (1) overcome the fraudster silencing you, and (2) go to a lawyer.

Chapter 1: Fraud Attorneys

There is a fraudster playbook complete with various ways to silence the potential whistleblower. At the extreme, the company fires you and reminds you of your confidentiality agreement in which you agreed not to share the inside happenings of the company. (These agreements are void against public policy when it comes to disclosing fraud as a whistleblower). The company may also get you to sign a release of claims. (These releases generally do not preclude you from bringing a whistleblower claim for fraud).

But often, the company silences the whistleblower in a more subtle way. This includes everyone around you confirming that the practice is perfectly fine. They make you feel like you don't know what you are talking about and can't be trusted to put 2 and 2 together. Someone tells you to keep your nose down and mind your own business. Or, they marginalize you by taking away responsibilities and excluding you from meetings. Most companies have a tight-knit culture. Everyone has stock options and is therefore financially at risk and incentivized to go with the flow. "Be a team player!" "Sweep the defects under the rug!" "It's no big deal."

Whistleblowers who make the decision to go against the flow and take a stand against the fraud have personal worries about coming forward to the government. One of the biggest is a having a relationship with the fraud. They participated. They sat in meetings where it was discussed and maybe sat silent. Fraud went on for months or years and they eventually signed off on it. Whistleblowers wonder, will I be prosecuted? Am I some sort of accomplice? Will I be fired if and when the company finds out who the whistleblower is? What exactly will happen when it is all brought to light?

A lawyer who is experienced in whistleblowing can make a world of difference to help ease the understandable stress whistleblowing can create. A good whistleblower lawyer will advise you if it is possible to remain anonymous as a whistleblower and will navigate the intricate waters of dealing with the government. He/she knows how to put a case together to maximize its appeal and present it to the government in the most valuable way. A good whistleblower lawyer also makes sure you are protected and will analyze pursing claims on your behalf if you have lost your job because you blew the whistle. But how do you choose a good lawyer?

V. What to Look for in a Lawyer

A. Experience

Whistleblowing is a complex area of the law. There are not very many lawyers who are experienced and have a record of success in the area. You want to find a lawyer with a track record of success, one who has built relationships with the government lawyers who will work on the case. You want a lawyer with a reputation with the government for being credible, straightforward, thorough and organized.

B. Trust

You want to find someone you can trust. Your lawyer will hear your secrets and advise you on the best way to proceed or, perhaps just as important, not to proceed. A good lawyer will assess your situation and advise you if there's something worth pursuing. A good lawyer will not only point out the good aspects of your case, but also the bad ones. I always find myself telling clients that there is no perfect case. A good lawyer who is thoughtful and genuine will point out the warts. Warts include details like: you eventually signed-off on the fraud, the documentation backing up your story is light, the theories of liability are complicated, the damages are hard to trace, or the materiality (*i.e.*, is this a big deal?) is questionable. The list goes on. If the case is worth pursuing, a good lawyer will know how to minimize and manage these imperfections.

C. Partnership

The best lawyers in these types of cases will make you feel an equal – like two partners in a business relationship. You will be the star witness for the fraud case, not your lawyer. You should partner with someone who brings out the best in you and makes you shine with expertise and credibility.

D. Ask Another Lawyer for A Referral

A great way to find a lawyer is to ask another lawyer for a referral to someone who does whistleblower work. Lawyers generally know who is good and are happy to refer you to the right person.

VI. What a Lawyer is Looking for in You

Lawyers who do this type of work typically take each case on a contingency basis. This means that they don't get paid unless you get paid. As the client, this means the lawyer shares the risk that there may not be any recovery. If there is no recovery from a settlement or judgment, you don't owe the lawyer anything as a fee for the time (usually hundreds of hours) spent on your case. As a result, good whistleblower lawyers only choose quality cases with good clients. You will be in a position to get a lawyer to take your case. A good way to look at this is the process of an audition.

It is crucial to find the client credible. Credibility is a mix of believability, sincerity, likeability, and motivation in coming forward. It is also about having the ability to tell the story in a clear and compelling way. Consider bringing documents to support what you allege. Think about corroborating witnesses. The more organized you are and the more you consider the roadmap of the fraud, the more credible you will be when telling the information to a lawyer (and the government).

Be prepared to say why you care about the fraud and why other people should care too. At the end of the day, what motivates you to come forward? What is the big picture? Is it patient safety, a misuse of taxpayer money, misleading shareholders, or protecting potential shareholders?

I always tell prospective clients they won't be able to surprise me. I have heard it all before. People are often in situations that seem fine (or at least doable) at the time, but, in hindsight, make up a pattern of fraudulent activities. In my experience, a company that cheats in one place cheats in others. There is usually more than just one thing, one time.

Use the protection of the attorney-client privilege. Tell your story to a lawyer (or two or three). Get it off your chest. Release the shame of having a secret, protected by the attorney-client privilege. The attorney will not, without your permission, be able to disclose what you told him/her about past activities. If anything, it will probably make you feel better just to tell someone.

Finally, be prepared to accept things that will be out of your control. Part of being a whistleblower demands working closely with the government. This means, at some point, you and your lawyer will hand the case (and thus the control) over to the government. Be prepared to accept the government will call many of the shots. Your lawyer will work to make sure the case is presented in the most valuable way, but at the end of the day, it will be the government making a lot of the decisions and this takes a lot of time. So, patience in the process is important.

VII. Doing the Right Thing Feels Good

Doing the right thing can create a sense of vindication – you knew what happened was wrong. Everyone around you tried to silence you but you stood up and someone paid attention and validated what you said.

Believe it or not, whistleblowers are good for corporate America. Companies are better off without fraud. It is a short-term strategy that is worse for the institution's reputation and stock price in the long run. In the end, companies and investors increase their loss when they choose fraud.

Blowing the whistle is also good for the government by allowing the government to recoup money lost to fraud or money as penalties for fraud. It makes the government a better spender, which is good for the 315 million of us in the country. Whistleblowers really are superheroes, and they should be rewarded with a good lawyer.

Doing the right thing can be hard. It goes against the tide. You are the little guy standing up to the giant. Doing the right thing involves courage, risk, and sometimes sacrifice. But blowing the whistle can be extremely rewarding – not only financially but also psychologically.

ABOUT THE AUTHOR

Carrie Mulholland Brous
Founder, Brous Law LLC
www.brouslaw.com
Tel: (913) 897-7877

Carrie Brous grew up in St. Louis, Missouri. She studied journalism at the University of Missouri and business at Sophia University in Tokyo, Japan. Carrie then returned to MU and graduated with highest honors at the top of her law school class in 1996. She lives in Prairie Village, Kansas, with her husband, three daughters and three dogs.

Carrie has over twenty years of experience representing both plaintiffs and defendants. After graduating, she practiced commercial law with Stinson Mag in Kansas City and St. Louis. In 2003, Carrie left Stinson and founded Brous Horn. For 12 years this firm successfully represented employees and whistleblowers in a myriad cases. In 2015, Carrie founded Brous Law where she remains committed to representing those seeking workplace justice and those who have been injured from drugs and medical devices. Carrie has an impressive case record of over $100 million in qui tam wins coupled with an individual "AV" rating by Martindale-Hubbell. For more information about Carrie, please visit brouslaw.com.

CHAPTER 2:
Family Attorneys

By: Jennifer Oswald Brown, Member, and
Erin Mayfield Craig, Domestic Attorney

I. Introduction

Dissolution of Marriage Actions and Modification of current decrees or judgments in Missouri are covered in most parts by the Missouri Revised Statutes. There are generally speaking four components of a dissolution of marriage: (1) custody of unemancipated children, (2) division of assets and debts, (3) maintenance, and (4) child support. These issues are complex and it is not advisable to navigate these issues without an attorney. Our domestic department has significant trial experience litigating family law matters, and considerable experience and knowledge in numerous other areas of law, including tax law, estate planning, wills and trusts, contract law, criminal law, corporate law and landlord-tenant law which are all intertwined with many aspects of family law cases. Before reading any of the following sections it is important to note that family law is highly fact specific and your certain set of circumstances will be unique. Therefore, it is important that your attorney is able to guide you through each step of the process depending upon the factors set forth below as well as applicable case law as it pertains to your particular case.

II. Filing of Pleadings for a Dissolution of Marriage Action

If you are filing a petition for a dissolution of marriage, you will need to make some basic allegations to the court in order for the court to obtain jurisdiction over the parties, minor children, and property and/or debt in your matter. First, if you ask the court for a dissolution of marriage, the pleading must be verified, signed by the party seeking relief, and the petition has to allege that the marriage is irretrievably broken and there is no reasonable likelihood that the marriage can be preserved. Also, the petition must contain the date of the marriage and the place that it is registered, the date of separation (if applicable), the current residences of each party, whether or not either party is on active duty with the armed forces of the United States, whether the wife is now pregnant, and that one of the parties has been a resident of Missouri for the 90 days preceding the filing of the action.

Additionally, if there are any children, you must list the children's names, ages, addresses, and where the children have resided for the past five years. The names of the child or children must be included so the court may make orders regarding their financial support and custody. A dissolution of marriage petition will need to request whether or not you are seeking maintenance. If you are requesting maintenance you will need to plead that you are without reasonable income or property to provide for your reasonable needs and that the other party is capable of providing support for yourself. Additionally, with any dissolution of marriage action, you need to ask the court for a fair and equitable division of your assets and debts, and/or if you enter into a property settlement agreement, that the property agreement is fair and not unconscionable. If you have children, you need to plead that the best interest of the children will be served by the parties sharing either joint or sole legal custody vested in one or both parties as well as joint or sole physical custody vested in one or both parties.

If you have been served a pleading for a dissolution of marriage, you must then file an answer within 30 days, or you are technically in default and the court, and upon hearing, the court may enter a judgment against you for failing to file a responsive pleading asking for affirmative relief. Thus, if you are served a pleading for a dissolution of marriage, you need to file an answer and counter-petition asking for the relief sought.

III. Division of Property and Debt - Dissolution of Marriage

The goal of the court in any dissolution proceeding is to equitably divide the parties' marital property and debts, which is not necessarily equally. Under Missouri's current dissolution of marriage statutes, there is a two-pronged approach the court will use to divide the assets and debts of a party. For each asset and debt, the court only has the authority to divide "marital property." Therefore, the court must first determine whether the asset or debt is a marital or non-marital asset or debt. The court does not have the discretion to divide non-marital property, and oftentimes disputes arise over what is considered non-marital property. However, marital v. non-marital property determination is not "black and white" because there are many ways that non-marital property can be converted to marital property, or develop a marital component, during a marriage. According to R.S.Mo. 452.330.2 non-marital property includes:

1. property acquired by gift, bequest, devise or descent;
2. property acquired in exchange for property acquired prior to the marriage or in exchange for property acquired by gift, bequest, devise or descent;
3. property acquired by a spouse after a decree of legal separation;
4. property excluded by a valid, written agreement of the parties (a prenuptial or postnuptial agreement); and
5. the increase in value of property acquired prior to the marriage or pursuant to the other above listed factors, unless marital assets, including the labor of the parties, have contributed to such increase, and then only to the extent of such contribution.

All property is considered marital until proven by clear and convincing evidence that the property is non-marital. Accordingly, if the other party contests that a piece of property is marital, they only have to raise the issue and you will have to prove that the property is non-marital. The Court will use what is known as the "source of funds" rule in determining what is a non-marital v. marital asset. A spouse that contributes to a non-marital asset is entitled to an interest in the asset to the extent that they have contributed to the value of the asset.

Additionally, if a non-marital asset has been comingled with a marital asset then the party claiming a portion of that asset is non-marital will have to trace out the portion that is non-marital. For example, if a party sells a non-marital asset for $5,000.00 and deposits the $5,000.00 into a joint account then the court will presume that the $5,000.00 is marital unless the party seeking to prove that it is non-marital can trace out the $5,000.00. Specifically, R.S.Mo. 452.330.4 states that property which would otherwise be non-marital property shall not become marital property solely because it is commingled with marital property. However, case law dictates that the passive increase in non-marital property retains its non-marital character, but the income from non-marital property is considered marital. This includes dividends and interest income. For example, a home that was bought and paid for before marriage is non-marital. Therefore, if the home increases $20,000.00 in value during the marriage, the $20,000.00 is considered non-marital still. Of course, even this has a caveat. If the $20,000.00 the home increased is due to any contribution from the other spouse, that spouse's contribution, or the marital contribution, is marital property. Therefore, if the home has increased $10,000.00 because a deck was added on by the other spouse's labor during the marriage, that $10,000.00 will be marital. Once property has been established as non-marital the burden shifts to the other spouse to prove that his/her contribution increased the value of the non-marital property.

In dividing marital property, the court will look to R.S.Mo. 452.330 to consider the relevant factors, which include:

1. The economic circumstances of each spouse at the time the

division of property is to become effective, including the desirability of awarding of awarding the family or home or the right to live therein for reasonable periods to the spouse having custody of any children;

2. The contribution of each spouse to the acquisition of the marital property, including the contribution of a spouse as homemaker;
3. The value of the non-marital property set apart to each spouse;
4. The conduct of the parties during the marriage; and
5. Custodial arrangements for minor children.

When analyzing the economic circumstances of each spouse at the time of the division of property, the court may consider awarding the home to the party that will have the children primarily in his/her care. Many different aspects of this intertwine with child custody. Generally speaking, the contribution of each spouse to the acquisition of the marital property is a fairly equal division, even if one party has contributed significantly more in a monetary value by way of income than another party.

Missouri is considered a modified no fault state. Therefore, Missouri courts can consider the conduct of the parties during the marriage. This factor centers more on "misconduct" rather than anything else. The misconduct must generally have some monetary component to it. For example, if a party was unfaithful during the marriage, the court will generally consider what monetary effect this had on the parties, such as expensive gifts given to the spouse's paramour or whether a spouses' conduct financially damaged the other spouse – such as accruing large gambling debts. However, it is important to consider that the court has the discretion not make any provisions relating to the misconduct of either party.

Remember that you always have the option to divide your property, both marital and non-marital outside of court with a Martial Settlement or Property Agreement. A Property Agreement can be filed with the court in which the parties request that the court to approve the agreement and make a finding that the agreement is fair and not unconscionable.

IV. Maintenance – Dissolution of Marriage

Maintenance is spousal support that is awarded in a dissolution or a legal separation case. If a party waives maintenance in a dissolution proceeding, he/she is forever barred from seeking maintenance in the future from his/her former spouse and he/she cannot come back to any court to obtain maintenance at any later time. Maintenance can be awarded by the court as modifiable or non-modifiable, per R.S.Mo. 452.335. However, case law provides that if the court awards maintenance it should be modifiable and should not dictate a specified time for the maintenance award to terminate. Thus, unless the party receiving maintenance remarries or the other party becomes deceased the maintenance order stays in effect until a court modifies or terminates the maintenance order upon the filing of a modification action. Remember that if you are agreeing to maintenance, you and your spouse can agree to a set amount and duration which becomes part of your judgment, and therefore an enforceable contract.

Maintenance is a two-step process in which the court must first decide: (1) whether the party seeking maintenance lacks sufficient property, including marital property apportioned to him/her to provide for his/her reasonable needs; and then additionally finds (2) that the spouse is unable to support himself/herself through appropriate employment or is the custodian of a child whose condition or circumstances make it appropriate that the custodian should not be required to seek employment outside the home. If the court finds both requirements are met, then the court may order an amount for a certain time period, sometimes without a time period, after considering the relevant factors set forth below, as set-forth in R.S.Mo. 452.335.

It is important to note that the court can take anything into consideration whenever awarding maintenance to either party, as long as the party seeking maintenance meets the first two threshold requirements. In making your case for or against maintenance, it is important to analyze past spending habits and the employment opportunities for each party. This is a process in which discovery will be the most helpful to your case including bank statements, employment records, and interrogatories or a deposition of the opposing party.

V. CHILD CUSTODY, PARENTING TIME OR VISITATION

Nothing inspires emotions and more controversial litigation than child custody issues. Child custody is guided by what Missouri statute and law has deemed the best interests of the child which is codified in R.S.Mo. 452.375. Custody takes two forms, legal and physical custody. Legal custody refers to decision making power of a party(ies) for the children and physical custody refers to parenting time or visitation shared between the parties.

Joint legal custody is the preferred custody arrangement in Missouri and is granted by the court upon a showing that the parties have the ability to confer and make an effort to make joint decisions with regards to their child(ren), in particular those related to major decisions effecting a child's health, education and general welfare. If a party is able to provide sufficient evidence to the court that he/she does not share a commonality of beliefs to make joint decisions in the best interest of a minor child the court may award sole legal custody to one party.

Similarly, there is a presumption for parties to share joint physical custody of their minor children. This means the parents will share parenting time, but not necessarily equal amounts of time. In order for a party to be granted sole physical custody, the evidence must support a "restriction" to the other party's time with the child, wherein that party's time is denominated as visitation. Recent case law provides that anything less than every other weekend and one night per week is a "restriction" on parenting time and thus considered sole physical custody to the parent who has the majority of time with the child. The courts use an eight-factor test, as set-forth in R.S.Mo. 452.375, to decide custodial arrangements.

VI. Child Support

Child support is in accordance with the guidelines set out in Rule 88.01, the Form 14, and R.S.Mo. 452.340. Child support decisions consider both the party receiving support and the party paying support's gross, not net, income. To determine credits on the Form 14, (child support worksheet) the Form 14 may take into consideration each party's respective percentage of income, credit to the parent providing health insurance for the minor child, reasonable childcare expenses and extraordinary costs of each child. Child support may be modified when the court finds that there is a change in circumstances so substantial as to make the terms of the current judgment unreasonable, among other factors.

VII. Modification of Prior Custody Order

modify the terms of your current parenting plan related to parenting time the court must find that there is a change in circumstances and that it is in the best interest of the child to modify the terms of your parenting plan based upon the eight (8) factors in R.S.Mo. 452.375. In order to modify an award of custody (e.g., from joint legal to sole legal custody), you must prove to the court (1) that the change in circumstances since the prior custody order is substantial regarding the minor child or other party and (2) the new custody order you are seeking is in the best interest of the minor child. Please note, modifications of custody and parenting time are subject to frequently changing case law and you and your attorney should rely on application of current case law when determining whether filing a modification would serve you and the child's best interest.

VIII. Paternity Actions

Paternity actions are initiated to establish a legal finding of a father/child relationship. There is a presumption of paternity if the alleged father's name appears on the child's birth certificate and he meets other criteria under Missouri law. However, this is merely a presumption and depending on the county in which the paternity action lies, it is not a legal finding of paternity. Thus, the presumed father will have no legal custody rights to the child unless or until otherwise ordered by the court.

IX. Relocation

When one party seeks to move (for over ninety days), he/she must give a relocation notice. This notice must be given to any party entitled to custody or visitation of the child and must be in writing by certified mail, return receipt requested. Absent "exigent circumstances" which the court would have to determine, written notice has to be provided at least sixty days in advance of the proposed relocation. For the specific requirements of what must be included in a relocation notice, see R.S.Mo. 452.377. In some instances, the court can waive these requirements. If you do not file a motion to prevent the relocation within thirty days of receiving the notice, the child may be relocated after sixty days. If a motion to prevent relocation is filed, the person seeking relocation must file a response to the motion within fourteen days setting forth the facts in support of the relocation and a revised parenting plan.

X. Family Access Motion

A party has the ability to file a family access motion, under R.S.Mo. 452.400, if your rights to custody, visitation, or third-party custody of a child/children under a judgment of dissolution, legal separation, or modification are denied or interfered with by a party without good cause. A family access is a simple, immediate remedy that can grant you compensatory time and can serve as a good way to get your judgment back on track.

XI. Conclusion

In conclusion, family law is complex and the case-law ever changing, always depending on the facts of each particular circumstance. We welcome the opportunity to speak with you regarding your specific case. What should first and foremost be considered by anyone that finds themselves looking at a dissolution of marriage, or any type of family action, is the safety of themselves and/or the minor children involved in the action. If you or your children are in danger of imminent harm, immediately seek the advice of an attorney about your options after ensuring the safety of yourself and your children.

ABOUT THE AUTHOR

Jennifer Oswald Brown
Partner, Oswald Roam
& Rew LLC
www.orrf-law.com
Tel: (816) 229-8121

Jennifer Oswald Brown received her BA from St. Louis University in 2008, and her JD from UMKC School of Law in 2001. Jennifer has been a member of Oswald Roam & Rew LLC since 2010, and prior to this has been a part of this firm since 2004. Jennifer focuses her practice in domestic and family law matters, which include dissolution of marriage, paternity and modifications. Jennifer also serves as serves as Court appointed Guardian ad Litem in Jackson, Lafayette, Cass, Ray, and Carroll Counties. Jennifer serves as a board member for the School of Economics, CAPA (Child Abuse Prevention Association), has recently been appointed to serve on the Missouri Supreme Court Combatting Human Trafficking & Domestic Violence Commission. Jennifer was honored and privileged to receive the 2016 Kelly J. Moorhouse Dedication to Children Award given by KCMBA for her contribution and dedication to representing children and families in the Greater Kansas City Area.

Special thanks and recognition go to Erin Mayfield-Craig for her efforts on this chapter. Erin is a family law attorney with the law firm Oswald Roam & Rew, LLC, and is admitted to the Missouri Bar.

CHAPTER 3:
Workers' Compensation Attorneys

By: Fred Bryant and Tom Bryant

I. Introduction

If you are injured on the job you may encounter a system that is new and foreign to you. All states have their own workers' compensation system. Each state system determines the rights an employee has under the law. Each state system also determines the obligations of the employee to qualify and/or apply for benefits under the law. Each state system also determines the rights, obligations, and defenses of the employer and/or its insurance company. While the workers' compensation system appears designed to protect injured workers, injured workers under the system soon realize that the system works to protect and limit the liability of their employer and their employers' insurance company. For that reason, it is important for you to know what your rights are and what is required of you to exercise those rights. The best way to understand your rights and obligations is to consult with a workers' compensation attorney. The questions below are those commonly asked by injured workers when confronted with the workers' compensation system. For purposes of this chapter we answered these commonly asked questions using Missouri workers' compensation law.

II. WHAT DO I DO IF I AM INJURED ON THE JOB?

If you are injured on the job, tell your supervisor and follow the procedures set forth by your employer for reporting work related injuries. It is important that you report your injury to your employer within thirty days or it may otherwise jeopardize your ability to receive workers' compensation benefits. Most employers will either take a report of injury orally or provide you with documentation to fill out. In any event, after completing the report of injury, please ask your employer to provide you a copy of that report. When reporting an injury be as specific as you can as to date, place, time of the injury and the specific description of how the injury occurred. Be sure to note any witnesses to the accident or incident that caused the injury. Keep track of the name of the person or persons to whom you reported the injury, as well as the date and time the injury was reported so you will have proof that in fact, the injury was reported.

If there is any delay in providing medical benefits after reporting the injury, it is wise to speak with an attorney experienced in practicing in the workers' compensation area.

III. DO I NEED AN ATTORNEY TO REPRESENT ME?

An attorney is not required on a workers' compensation case. However, a workers' compensation case is a legal proceeding. The employer, either on its own or through its workers' compensation insurance carrier, has legal representation. The Administrative Law Judge assigned to the case cannot provide legal advice or act as an adviser to either side.

In many instances, when the injury is relatively minor such as a cut requiring stitches and where there is little or no missed work and little or no medical treatment, the injured worker may decide that he/she does not need a lawyer to represent him/her.

Attorneys who regularly practice in the workers' compensation area offer free initial consultation. These attorneys represent injured workers on a "contingent fee" basis meaning they are not paid until the case is resolved and the fee is based on a percentage of the settlement or award. In Missouri, the contingency fee of the employee's attorney must be approved by the Administrative Law Judge assigned to the case. It cannot exceed 25% of the total settlement award.

Since consultations with workers' compensation attorneys are free and any fee is not paid until the end of the case and must be approved by the judge, you should, at the very least, call and talk with an attorney after an injury on the job. It is particularly important to make sure your rights to the benefits available under the Missouri Workers' Compensation law are understood and protected since the trend in recent law changes is to limit the rights of the injured worker. Because of these changes in the law, more and more workers have their case denied at the outset and have medical benefits denied and temporary payments while they are off work withheld.

We recommend that you should at the very least consult and seriously consider hiring a lawyer when the following situations develop:

1. Your employer denies your claim or fails to provide medical or wage loss benefits promptly. If you are injured on the job, report your injury and your employer and its insurance company fail to provide medical care or pay benefits while you are off work due to the injury, you need to consult a lawyer.

2. If your employer wrongfully withholds medical treatment, it may be found responsible for all medical costs you incur treatment of the injury. In addition, an attorney may file certain proceedings with the Workers' Compensation Division so that your case can be promptly heard on the medical benefits issue.

3. If the settlement offer by your employer or its insurance company doesn't seem fair, you need to consult with a lawyer to make sure you receive the benefits to which you are entitled. While settlements must have judicial approval, the judge cannot give specific advice to the employee as to whether the proposed settlement adequately provides for you.

4. If your medical issues prevent you from returning to your prior

job or from performing any work at all, you may be entitled to the permanent total disability which could involve lifetime weekly benefits to make up for your loss of employment. These types of cases are complex and require evidence from medical and vocational experts as to the nature and extent of your disability and why the disability prevents you from returning to the work force. These cases potentially involve substantial benefits and will be hotly contested by the employer and its insurance carriers because of that fact. An experienced workers' compensation lawyer recognizes and develops the medical and vocational evidence needed on a case involving the seriousness of the loss of job and ability to work.

5. If you receive Social Security Disability benefits, your workers' compensation settlement may affect those benefits. Social Security may be entitled to a large portion of your workers' compensation benefits and an attorney experienced in practicing under workers' compensation law knows how to draft and negotiate the settlement agreement to minimize or eliminate the offset of Social Security benefits.

6. If your employer discriminates or retaliates against you for the filing of a workers' compensation case by firing you, demoting you, cutting your hours, reducing your pay or in other ways making the workplace a hostile environment, you should consult an attorney to protect both your workers' compensation and civil rights. For example, in the State of Missouri, and most other states, there are specific laws protecting the injured worker from discrimination because of exercising their rights under the workers' compensation law. In Missouri, any employer or its agent who discharges or in any way discriminates against you for exercising your workers' compensation rights is subject to a civil suit for damages by you. Currently, the law requires you to demonstrate your workers' compensation claim was a contributing factor to the discrimination. A lawyer experienced in the workers' compensation area can, in some cases, prevent discrimination by the employer by

Chapter 3: Workers' Compensation Attorneys

threatening to file a civil action for damages or may be able to pursue such a lawsuit if the employer persists in retaliating against you for filing a workers' compensation claim.

7. If your injury on the job was caused by a third-party, you may have a civil action against that negligent third-party in addition to your workers' compensation case. For example, if you are injured on the job by a negligent motorist, you have a civil claim against the negligent motorist, in addition to receiving workers' compensation benefits. An experienced workers' compensation attorney can maximize your recovery against both the employer in the workers' compensation setting and the negligent third-party in the civil setting.

8. An attorney is familiar with all the deadlines on a claim, the evidence needed to make a claim, and how to maximize the value of a claim to include the possibility of ongoing or future medical for the injury.

Many employees are hesitant to hire an attorney as they are worried about the fees, costs, and receiving less than if they had represented themselves. In Missouri, the Division of Workmens' Compensation conducted a survey and found that for those employees with attorneys, their results were 38% higher than those employees who were unrepresented.

Injured employees are best served when they fully understand their rights and protections afforded them under the law. You are encouraged to consult with an attorney who is experienced in practicing in the area of workers' compensation.

IV. WHAT BENEFITS AM I ENTITLED TO?

While each state's benefits differ, three benefits exist in most every state system. The three most common benefits are medical treatment, benefits while off work due to injury (commonly referred to as temporary total disability benefits), and a final monetary settlement or award commonly referred to as permanent partial disability or impairment benefits.

A. MEDICAL TREATMENT

Most workers' compensation systems provide you with medical treatment for you work related injury or occupational illness. In the state of Missouri, the law requires your employer to provide medical treatment and you can choose the medical providers who provide that treatment. The employer or its workers' compensation carrier must pay for this medical treatment. You may select your own medical provider rather than the providers selected by your employer/insurer but if you do so, you are responsible for the cost of the treatment.

Often disputes regarding medical treatment arise. In Missouri, there are procedures that allow you to seek additional treatment after being denied or released from care.

B. TEMPORARY TOTAL DISABILITY BENEFITS

In Missouri, temporary total disability benefits are benefits paid to you on a weekly basis when you are off from work due to your injury/ medical restrictions. If the treating medical provider states that you should be kept off work then the employer/work compensation insurance company is responsible to pay monetary benefits. Sometimes a treating medical provider may provide you with restrictions. If the employer cannot accommodate the restrictions then you are also entitled to temporary total disability benefits.

The temporary total disability benefits in Missouri equal two-thirds your gross (non-tax) weekly wage. The benefit amount is capped based on the year the injury occurred. You are entitled to the lesser of: (1) two-thirds of your gross average weekly wage or (2) the cap. It is important to note that these benefits are tax exempt in Missouri.

C. PERMANENT PARTIAL DISABILITY BENEFITS

If your workers' compensation injury leads to a permanent disability you may be entitled to a final monetary settlement that is sometimes referred to as permanent partial disability or impairment benefit. States differ greatly on how they determine what the final settlement permanent disability or impairment is. However, most of the time the value is guided by opinions given by the treating medical doctors and other medical experts.

In Missouri, permanent total disability benefits are determined by using this formula: *(Body part injured)* **X** *(% of disability assigned) X (2/3 weekly wage) = Final Settlement.* Again, the weekly wage is capped so you are entitled to the lesser of: (1) 2/3 your gross average weekly wage or (2) the cap.

In Missouri, the body part injured portion of the formula is determined by looking at the Missouri statutes which provide a number of weeks for each particular body part. Here are the Missouri numbers based on the body part:

Body as Whole (including neck & back)	400 weeks
Shoulder	232 weeks
Upper Arm (from elbow to shoulder)	222 weeks
Elbow	210 weeks
Forearm	200 weeks
Wrist/Hand	175 weeks
Thumb (1st or Proximal Joint)	60 weeks
Thumb (2nd or Distal Joint)	45 weeks
1st Finger (1st or Proximal Joint)	45 weeks
1st Finger (2nd Joint)	35 weeks
1st Finger (3rd or Distal Joint)	30 weeks
2nd Finger (1st or Proximal Joint)	35 weeks
2nd Finger (2nd Joint)	30 weeks
2nd Finger (3rd or Distal Joint)	26 weeks
3rd Finger (1st or Proximal Joint)	35 weeks
3rd Finger (2nd Joint)	30 weeks
3rd Finger (3rd or Distal Joint)	26 weeks
4th Finger (1st or Proximal Joint)	22 weeks
Hip/Thigh	207 weeks
Knee	160 weeks

Calf (ankle to knee)	155 weeks
Ankle	150 weeks
Foot	110 weeks
Complete Loss of Sight	140 weeks (one eye)
Complete Deafness	180 weeks (both ears)
(one ear)	49 weeks

The next part of the formula, percentage of disability, is assigned by a medical provider. Doctors sometimes disagree as to the percentage of disability. Many times, the employer will ask the treating physician to provide the percentage. You can hire a medical expert to provide a percentage of disability.

The last part of the formula is the wage rate. The wage rate is determined, in Missouri, by taking two-thirds your weekly wage. The weekly wage does have a maximum rate which is determined by the year of your injury.

Let's say for example that you injured your shoulder at work on January 15, 2016 and were making $1,200 a week. If the treating doctor assigned a 10% disability you would be entitled to $10,778.25 as your settlement. The formula would look like this:

232 weeks for the shoulder X 10% disability X $464.58 = $10,778.25.

V. WILL I BE ABLE TO RECOVER FOR MY PAIN AND SUFFERING?

Generally, a recovery specifically for pain and suffering in a workers' compensation claim is not allowed. This is because the workers' compensation system is based almost entirely upon the nature and extent of the disability suffered to the injured body part as a result of the work-related accident/or occupational disease. The primary benefits under the workers' compensation system are medical benefits, wage loss benefits (called temporary total disability) while you are off work from injury and permanent partial disability benefits for the nature and extent of the disability sustained by you from the injury. You may also be entitled to future medical benefits in certain circumstances.

While pain and suffering may be a component or factor in measuring your disability, no money is awarded under the workers' compensation system for pain and suffering. You may receive an award of future medical prescriptions to help control pain and pain itself may affect range of motion and physical activities in connection with the work which would have an impact on the degree of disability. However, the fact that an injury caused pain or may continue to be painful after treatment is not compensated under the workers' compensation system.

VI. Who Do I Bring My Workers' Compensation Claim Against?

The claim for workers' compensation benefits is generally brought against your employer. If your employer purchased workers' compensation insurance, the insurance company, or its attorneys, will defend the claim. Some larger employers self-insure, meaning they defend and pay their own claims.

VII. What State Can I Bring My Claim In?

Workers' compensation jurisdiction is important since each workers' compensation system is different. Tt is important for you to bring your workers' compensation claim in the state that benefits you the most. In some instances, a workers' compensation claim can be brought in two separate states simultaneously.

In Missouri, a claim under the workers' compensation system can be made in the state if the injury occurred in Missouri, your principal place of employment is in Missouri, or you and your employer had a contract for employment in Missouri.

A situation that is common in Kansas City, Missouri, because we sit so close to the Missouri and Kansas state line, is when a Missouri employee for a Missouri employer is injured performing a job in the state of Kansas or vice versa. In this situation, you would likely have the right to file the claim in both states. The purpose to filing workers' compensation claims in both states is not to recover two separate settlements for the same claim, but is used to protect you by allowing the choice to proceed under the state law that provides you the most protection and greatest amount of benefits.

VIII. What is a Claim for Compensation?

A Claim for Compensation is the formal filing of your work-related injury with the Division of Workers' Compensation. The Division of Workers' Compensation is the state agency charged with administering your workers' compensation claim. Administrative Law Judges working for the Division of Workers' Compensation are the judges who oversee your claim and make decisions on your claim.

You must file your Claim for Compensation within the time allowed by law or the claim is time barred regardless of the merits of the claim. In Missouri, the statute of limitations for filing of a claim is two years from the date of accident or two years from the date of last payment, whichever is later. The last payment would be payments made by the employer and/or its insurance carrier for medical or payments while you are off work. If the employer fails to file a report of injury with the Division of Workers' Compensation, the time to file the claim may be extended to three years from date of accident.

The Claim for Compensation is like filing of a lawsuit in a civil case because it formally notifies the Division of Workers' Compensation, the employer, and its insurance carrier that you are bringing a formal claim for compensation for all the benefits to which you may be entitled under the workers' compensation law.

IX. What if I Can't Return to My Job?

The answer to this question differs greatly from state to state. Some workers' compensation systems award different types of damages if you are unable to return to the *type* of work you did before. For example, in Kansas the workers' compensation system has a claim called work disability for those that cannot perform the same or similar job tasks.

Under Missouri, law your permanent partial disability rating may be affected because you are unable to return to your job. However, there is no additional claim if you are unable to return to your job unless you are unable to return to *any type* of employment. Under Missouri law then, the focus is not whether you can return to your prior job but whether you can return to any employment.

X. What if I Can't Work Again?

If you cannot work again you may be entitled to permanent total disability benefits. Under Missouri law, you entitled to permanent total disability benefits if you cannot return to *any* employment. This is a very high standard because employers and insurance companies will claim there are jobs you can perform even if you have not done that type of work in your employment history. The employer/insurer doesn't have to place you in a job, merely show there are jobs in the labor force you can perform.

If you do qualify for permanent total disability benefits under Missouri law you are entitled to two-thirds you weekly wage (maxed at the applicable rate) on a weekly basis for your entire life. Instead of receiving two-thirds your weekly wage for life each week you can negotiate a lump sum settlement.

XI. Am I Entitled to a Trial by Jury?

No. Workers' Compensation in the state of Missouri is an administrative system. The structure of the system is set up so that there are no jury trials. Many times in workers' compensation cases, you, with counsel, can settle certain disputes with the employer/insurance company without the need for a final hearing. However, if the disputes in the case cannot be settled you have a right to a hearing before an Administrative Law Judge. The Administrative Law Judge will render a final decision in your case. In the state of Missouri, Administrative

Law Judges only handle workers' compensation cases so they are very familiar with the issues and relevant case law.

Should you disagree with the decision of the Administrative Law Judge, you have a right to appeal your decision to the Missouri Department of Labor and Industrial Relations ("Commission"). The Commission is a three-person panel that will conduct a *de novo* review of the Administrative Law Judges' decision. A *de novo* review means the Commission will look at the trial transcript and all evidence admitted at hearing and will make its own independent decision on the case. It is not bound by or obligated to follow the findings of the Administrative Law Judge. In Missouri, you have an absolute right to appeal the Administrative Law Judge's decision to the Commission.

Should you disagree with the decision of the Commission you may decide to appeal the case to the Missouri Court of Appeals. At the Missouri Court of Appeals level, the court only reviews the case to determine whether the law was properly applied to the facts as found by the Commission. It does not rehear the facts as found by the Commission. If there is disagreement with the decision of the Missouri Court of Appeals, you may seek and appeal to the Missouri Supreme Court. The Missouri Supreme court decides which cases it chooses to hear.

It is important to note that the employer/insurance company has the same rights to appeal decisions as you do.

XII. CAN I BRING A WORKERS' COMPENSATION CLAIM AND SUE A THIRD-PARTY FOR ITS NEGLIGENT CONDUCT?

A very common situation often encountered if you are injured on the job, is when you are injured by another party that is not associated with your employer. The most common example of this situation is if you are driving for work and are involved in an automobile collision. You, because you were on the job, would likely have a right to bring a workers' compensation claim. You could also pursue a negligence claim against the other negligent driver. The claim against the employer falls within the workers' compensation system. The claim against the negligent driver is a civil claim. Two separate claims exist and each claim seeks different damage categories.

Since you cannot recover for pain and suffering under Missouri workers' compensation law, you can claim such damages against the negligent driver.

Under the automobile collision example above you maintain two separate claims and can recover two separate settlements. Under Missouri law, it is likely best for you to pursue your workers' compensation claim first and then pursue your third-party claim against the negligent party. Timing is important under Missouri law because the workers' compensation employer/insurance company may have a right of reimbursement from the third-party settlement for some of the benefits previously paid out. Practically, this means that while you can have both a workers' compensation settlement or award and a third-party settlement or verdict, you may have to pay back some of the third-party settlement or verdict to your employer or its workers' compensation insurance company.

XIII. CONCLUSION

You deserve the benefits you are entitled under workers' compensation law. While this chapter attempted to answer some of the more frequently asked questions by injured workers, each case has its own unique circumstances and facts. This chapter is not a substitute for contacting an attorney experienced in handling workers' compensation cases should you have any questions about your rights and protections under the law.

ABOUT THE AUTHORS

Frederick W. Bryant
Partner, The Bryant Law Firm
www.bryantlawkc.com
Tel: (816) 221-0350

Frederick W. Bryant ("Fred") is a founding member of The Bryant Law Firm. Fred has spent his entire 37 year career representing injured individuals in personal injury matters and injured workers in workers compensation matters. Fred is a member of the Kansas City Metropolitan Bar Association where he is a member of the Workers Compensation Committee. He is also a member of the Missouri Association of Trial Attorneys where he was elected to the Board of Governors in 2005 and continues to serve in that capacity. He is a member of the American Association of Justice, a national organization dedicated to the rights of injured individuals in the civil justice system. Fred is a Missouri State Delegate to that organization. Fred is also a member of the Workers Injury Law & Advocacy Group.

Thomas P. Bryant
Partner, The Bryant Law Firm
www.bryantlawkc.com
Tel: (816) 221-0350

Tom Bryant is a founding member of The Bryant Law Firm. Tom practices in the area of personal injury litigation for individuals and worker's compensation for the injured worker. Tom has handled civil and worker's compensation matters from trial through the appellate process in both Kansas and Missouri. Tom was named a Rising Star in Missouri by Super Lawyers Magazine. Tom is a member of the Kansas City Metropolitan Bar Association, Clay County Bar Association, Missouri Association of Trial Attorneys and American Association of Justice.

CHAPTER 4:
Employment Attorneys

By: Isaac D. Keppler

I. Introduction

Choosing the right attorney for your employment issue will often be the difference between a satisfactory resolution and unfavorable result. Many individuals encountering an employment-related legal issue for the first time will mistakenly believe that a quick call to an attorney will fix the problem. In reality, choosing an attorney should be a thoughtful and deliberate process that will require work on your part.

We recommend several steps and considerations when choosing an employment attorney, such as: (a) gain an understanding of the issue you face and consider your goal; (b) choose an attorney who focuses on employment law and has experience with your specific issue; and (c) evaluate the overall experience and reputation of the attorneys you are considering. If you are an aggrieved employee, consider (a) contacting and using an attorney who is a member of the National Employment Lawyers Association ("NELA"); (b) accessing publicly available court records to learn which attorneys have litigated against your specific employer; and (c) meet with attorneys, ask questions, and gauge your comfort level with their competence and style.

II. Understand Your Issue and Consider Your Goals

Before you begin actively seeking an employment attorney you should take some time to understand the issue you face and the goal you want to achieve. For example, are you about to begin a new employment relationship? If so, are you negotiating the terms of an employment contract? Have you been asked to sign a non-competition agreement and want to know what the agreement provides? Have you recently been let go from a job and believe you were fired for an illegal reason? Or perhaps, you are a manager or supervisor and have been informed that you are under investigation and need guidance on your rights and responsibilities.

Whatever your specific issue may be, you will be much better prepared to engage an attorney if you first develop a clear understanding of the facts at issue and a basic understanding of the goals you want to achieve.

While it may sound obvious, it can be helpful to jot down the facts as soon as you decide that you might need an attorney. This will help guide you in your selection process and allow you to educate potential attorneys quickly.

III. Choose from Attorneys Who Focus on Employment Law and Have Experience with Your Specific Issue

Once you have factually identified your employment issue, you are in a good position to research attorneys who you may want to meet. Keep in mind, employment law is a vast body of law. Employment-related laws and regulations evolve quickly and are filled with nuance. For this reason, many attorneys focus their entire law practice on specific niche areas, such as wage and hour claims or employee discrimination and retaliation.

When researching, you should focus your efforts on attorneys who regularly practice in employment law and who have experience in the specific area of law where you require assistance.

When employment issues arise, we often see employers and defendants turn to the attorney who they "used before" for other, non-employment law issues. There is great value in having an attorney you know and trust who you can call on short notice. However, when non-employment lawyers handle matters outside their general knowledge and experience, we often see undesirable results such as the escalation of a situation that could have been resolved earlier, unintentionally creating or enhancing claims through ill-advised responses, and a significant increase in legal costs and fees.

Similarly, when an employee or potential plaintiff hires an attorney who does not have employment law experience, the individual is often left with unrealistic expectations about the value or viability of his or her case, and the matter often stalls out or loses momentum without a clear resolution.

For these reasons, it is best to limit your research to attorneys who practice employment law generally and have experience with your specific area of need. When you begin your research, it might be difficult to distinguish between attorneys who actually practice employment law, and attorneys who have specialty practices related to employment, such as worker's compensation attorneys or attorneys who specialize in unemployment appeals. You should be aware that all states, and most metropolitan areas, have an attorney bar association that can refer attorneys based on practice area. If you are overwhelmed by the amount of information retrieved from a basic internet search, local bar associations can be a great resource for locating attorneys who primarily handle employment law. Two referral sources in the greater metropolitan Kansas City area are the Johnson County Bar Association (http://www.jocobar.org/) and the Kansas City Metropolitan Bar Association (https://www.kcmba.org/).

IV. Overall Experience and Reputation Matter

When selecting an employment attorney, you should always consider the attorney's overall experience and reputation. On the topic of experience, you should ask how many years has the attorney been practicing and how many of those years have been dedicated to employment law? Typically, a more experienced attorney will have a greater breadth of knowledge, and has probably dealt with a situation like yours many times. Experienced attorneys may also have more established relationships with other local attorneys which can allow a more efficient and effective negotiation process.

Candidly, the issue of attorney experience often involves a potential compromise. More experienced attorneys often charge more per hour or are very selective about cases they accept. They also may have less available time to dedicate to your case. So, if you need a lot of attorney contact it may be difficult or expensive with an experienced. On the other hand, while a less experienced attorney may not be able to draw upon the same depth of experience, he or she may be more willing to invest time and resources into your case. Often, less experienced attorneys are willing to take on difficult cases and pursue more novel theories. Consequently, when selecting an employment attorney, you want to find the best balance of an attorney who is experienced, but also available to meet the needs of your case.

An attorney's reputation often goes hand-in-hand with his or her experience. Ask around. Does the attorney have a reputation for clear, timely communication? Does the attorney achieve satisfactory results for the client more often than not? Does the attorney have a reputation for candor and integrity? Answers to these questions will directly bear on the results you may achieve. Attorneys who have a good reputation with other attorneys and judges typically achieve better results for their clients than those who do not. One easy way to find information about many attorneys' reputations is by searching websites such as Martindale-Hubbell (https://www.martindale.com). Martindale-Hubbell is an easy website to navigate. Websites like Martindale-Hubbell typically provide free information, and create attorney reviews based upon an attorney's reputation for skill, ethics, integrity, and other categories that are important to your consideration.

V. Plaintiff-Specific Considerations

If you are considering legal action against a current, former, or prospective employer, there are a couple resources you should consult. NELA is an association of attorneys who are dedicated to representing plaintiff-employees in employment-related issues. NELA has a strong network of participating attorneys so you will typically find NELA associated attorneys in any given region. NELA attorneys typically share tips and strategies with one another which tends to provide better results for their clients. You can find information about NELA and locate participating attorneys at https://www.nela.org/.

Additionally, if you are considering legal action against a specific company or business, you should consult local, publicly available, court records to find out whether the company has been sued for similar issues in the past. If so, the attorney(s) who handled the previous case will often have a wealth of information about the company's litigation tactics, settlement ranges, appetite for risk, and other information that can be very helpful. For example, in Johnson County, Kansas, many court records are accessible through https://www.jococourts.org/ which provides access to the public records for the Johnson County, Kansas District Court. In the Missouri state court system, you may obtain court records by logging on to https://www.courts.mo.gov/casenet. And, for cases filed in federal courts across the county you may obtain public court filings by creating an account at https://www.pacer.gov/ which is federal government's electronic system allowing public access to electronic court records. It is an extremely useful tool.

VI. Meeting with Attorneys

After you complete your background research, you should schedule a meeting with one or more attorneys to discuss the facts and issues of your case. This meeting is critical in your selection process. Be prepared and attentive. Ask issue specific questions, and pay attention to the response. The attorney should be able to describe the basic process that applies to your specific employment issue and explain how he or she handled similar issues in the past. If your case involves an issue of discrimination or retaliation, you may be required to file a charge with an administrative agency as a prerequisite to filing a lawsuit. Did the attorney adequately explain this process to you?

During the meeting, you should ask about budgeting and overall cost. These costs will vary widely, particularly since some attorneys will handle plaintiffs' matters on a contingency fee basis.

You should ask questions about the results you might achieve in your case. This will help you value the investment of time and resources you are likely to put into your case, and evaluate whether the attorney's views are compatible with your own.

During this meeting, you should ask yourself whether you are comfortable with the attorney's style and demeanor. In most matters, you will work closely with the attorney for many hours. Is this a person you are comfortable working with? You should also ask the attorney who will work on your case. You may be comfortable with the attorney in the initial meeting, but if that attorney passes the case to someone else and is not involved in your case, then your selection process will be undermined.

Finally, during your meeting you should ask the attorney to provide examples of results in similar cases. A good employment attorney should be willing to give general information about a range of results they achieved in cases like yours.

VII. Conclusion

We recognize that when you face an employment-related legal matter, you may not have the time and resources to conduct a detailed analysis of prospective attorneys. However, by expending additional time and effort at the beginning, you will be in position to make a much more informed decision about hiring an attorney, and in most cases, your choice of attorney will be one of the most significant factors in whether you achieve a satisfactory result.

ABOUT THE AUTHOR

Isaac D. Keppler
Associate,
Colantuono Bjerg Guinn, LLC
www.ksmolaw.com
Tel: (913) 345-2555

Isaac D. Keppler, of the firm Colantuono Bjerg Guinn, LLC., is an experienced litigator, negotiator, and advisor. He represents clients in both state and federal court and before administrative agencies. Isaac regularly counsels clients on matters involving routine hiring and firing, payroll and FLSA compliance, ADA and GINA/ADEA/FMLA/Title VII discrimination, retaliation and harassment issues, employment contracts, noncompetition agreements, and a variety of human resources, employee management, and other business issues. Isaac is admitted to practice in Kansas, Missouri and Idaho. He is an active member of the Earl E. O'Connor Inn of Court and the Johnson County Bar Association. He regularly contributes an employment law advice column to the Bar Letter for the Johnson County Bar Association.

Isaac graduated from Western New England University School of Law in 2007. Prior to joining Colantuono Bjerg Guinn, LLC, Isaac worked as a litigation attorney for a mid-sized litigation and business firm in Boise, Idaho. Isaac clerked for a state district court judge and worked as a research and writing attorney for the Kansas Supreme Court.

CHAPTER 5:
Taxation Attorneys

By: Zachary Goff

I. Introduction

Taxation is an ever changing and important area of the law which, in one way or another, affects all our lives in many ways. Tax touches on nearly every aspect of our lives and, in some way, on every other area of law. Taxes are ever present, but not understood. Nearly everything we do in our daily lives results in some tax consequence or, at least, the thought "I wonder what this will do to my taxes?". In a broad sense, whether it is larger events like selling a house, having children, changing jobs, buying a car, a parent dying, or smaller events such as putting the kids in daycare or travelling out of town for work, all have specific tax consequences of some sort. Also, I use the term "consequences" to refer to both positive and negative situations. Whether a particular situation increases or decreases your tax due, the situation has a "consequence."

II. Taxing Authorities in the United States

There are many levels of government in the United States and each has its own authority to assess tax upon those living or doing business within its jurisdiction. For example, if you live in Kansas City, Missouri, you will pay tax to the City of Kansas City (earnings tax and sales taxes), Jackson County (sales taxes, property taxes), the

State of Missouri (income tax and sales tax), and the U.S. Treasury (excise taxes on products such as gasoline and, most famously, the Federal Income Tax). Although the rates and types of taxes may vary at the local, county, and state levels, this is generally true for every person living in an American city.

The focus of this chapter is the Federal Income Tax – as it is applied to individuals – and some state matters. I will also discuss what steps you must take if you receive a notice from the Internal Revenue Service and some of the options available to you during the audit or collection process.

III. HISTORY OF THE INCOME TAX

The income tax has been around for over 100 years despite efforts to enact it during periods much earlier than this. Why was there such difficulty in enacting the code? A graduated income tax in the form we currently have was determined by the Supreme Court to violate the original provisions of the Constitution. Article I, Section 8 of the U.S. Constitution provides that "Congress shall have the power to lay and collect Taxes, Duties, Imposts and Excises . . . ." Article I, Section 2 further provides that "Representatives and direct Taxes shall be apportioned among the several States which may be included within this Union . . . ." This section is known as the Apportionment Clause which restricts Congress' authority under Article I, Section 8 to pass bills to lay and collect taxes. It is this references to "direct tax" and "apportionment" among the states that caused some fundamental issues the development of the income tax in the United States.

The term "direct tax" is not defined in the Constitution and its interpretation was left to the courts. In 1796, the Supreme Court was called to decide *Hylton v. United States*, a case which covered a yearly carriage tax. In this case, which Alexander Hamilton argued before the Court in favor of the tax, the Court determined that the carriage tax was not a "direct tax" as contemplated by the Constitution and, therefore, did not require apportionment. The Court essentially viewed all taxes on land as a "direct tax" and all other taxes as not direct taxes. This case served as precedent for nearly 100 years.

In 1862, based on the *Hylton* decision, Congress passed the Revenue Act of 1861 which introduced America's first income tax. In 1894, Congress passed the Wilson-Gorman Tariff Act which provided a tax on any "gains, profits and incomes" - including dividends from stock - in excess of $4,000. The Farmers' Loan & Trust Company told its shareholders that it would pay the tax on behalf of its shareholders. Charles Pollock, a shareholder of the Famers' Loan & Trust Company, objected to the Company paying the tax and brought suit in lower courts.

Mr. Pollock's case, *Pollock v. Farmers' Loan and Trust Company*, reached the Supreme Court. The Supreme Court held that the taxes levied by the Wilson-Gorman Tariff Act were unconstitutional. The Court found that since the tax was levied on income from property (in this case company stock) it should be considered a "direct tax." Since it is a direct tax it must be "apportioned" among the states. This apportionment was not accounted for in the Wilson-Gorman Tariff Act therefore, the Court held, the tax was unconstitutional. Thus, the *Pollock* Court extended the *Hylton* Court's decision that all taxes on income from land (taxing rents) was a direct tax to include taxes on income from personal property (dividends, interest, capital gains). The *Pollock* decision was not a very popular one among the populist movement of the time because it excluded the primary income sources of the very rich from the income tax.

Following *Pollock* President Taft, in 1909, proposed the Sixteenth Amendment to the Constitution. The Sixteenth Amendment states:

> The Congress shall have the power to lay and collect taxes on incomes, from whatever source derived, without apportionment among the several States, and without regard to any census or enumeration.

The Amendment was passed by three-fourths of state legislatures on February 25, 1913, and the *Pollock* decision was overturned. Soon thereafter, Congress passed the first modern national income tax act into law and taxes on income from property no longer needed to be apportioned.

Many interesting decisions followed that rejected taxpayer arguments that the income tax exceeded Congress' power focusing on some other Article or Amendment of the Constitution. Notably, the *Brushaber* case decided in 1916 ruled that the income tax laws do not violate the Fifth Amendment's prohibition against the government taking property without due process of law. This is an argument that taxpayers attempt to argue even today. The Internal Revenue Service ("IRS") and the Tax Court consider this argument, along with several others, frivolous. Taxpayers attempting to put forth this argument in Tax Court are subject to additional sanctions (in addition to losing their case).

The final bit of historical information included in this Chapter is the seminal case which provided us with the modern interpretation of income. The Sixteenth Amendment states that Congress may tax incomes "from whatever source derived." In 1955, *Commissioner v. Glenshaw Glass Co.*, was decided and is the judicial source for our understanding of income and the sources therefrom derived. This case holds that

> the statutory term, "gross income," encompasses "accessions to wealth, clearly realized, and over which the taxpayers have complete dominion." This essentially means that any action that increases your wealth will have an income tax consequence unless that source is specifically excluded by Congress.

For example, wages earned and capital gains from the sale of stock or real estate result in income. But gifts, life insurance proceeds and unrealized appreciation of stock and real estate are not included in your income even though they clearly increase your wealth. Gifts and life insurance proceeds are excluded from income by section 102 and 101, respectively, of the Internal Revenue Code of 1986, as amended ("Code").

IV. The Source of Tax Law

The Code, contains all the Federal tax laws in the United States. Court cases, Department of the Treasury regulations, and IRS pronouncements merely serve as interpretations of the Code's provisions. The Code is found in Title 26 of the United States Code. There are thousands of sections of revenue statutes found within Title 26. To provide some organization to this mass of laws, Title 26 is organized into Subtitles, Chapters, Subchapters, Parts and Sections. Each level getting more detailed in its provisions.

The Federal Income Tax is found exclusively in Title 26, Subtitle A, Chapters 1-6. These six chapters consist of 1,564 sections of income tax law applicable to individuals, corporations, partnerships, estates and trusts. Other Title 26 Subtitles of note are: (1) Subtitle B - Estate Tax and Gift Taxes, (2) Subtitle C – Employment Taxes, and Subtitle F – Procedure and Administration. A thorough understanding of the organization and application of each Chapter and Subchapter found in Title A is necessary to understanding income taxes.

V. Gross Income

The fundamental starting point for calculating income tax liability is some calculation of gross income. Code Section 61 defines "gross income" as a concept and follows the concept of the Sixteenth Amendment and *Glenshaw Glass Co.* The concept of gross income addressed above is not only the proper starting point in income tax education, it is the first concept addressed when completing every tax return. For example, lines 7 through 22, the first lines requiring actual numbers, of Form 1040 are geared toward properly calculating gross income for the year. Just to add unwelcome confusion it is referred to as "Total Income" on the form but the concept derives from gross income. Some lines in the Income section of Form 1040 are relatively easy to calculate. Others, such as Line 17 reporting income from partnerships, S corporations, trusts, etc., may require completing an entirely different, and more complex, income tax form (i.e., Forms 1065, 1120-S or 1041) before inserting the one number required for line 17.

A. Adjustments to Gross Income to arrive at AGI

The next step in completing the tax return are the adjustments or deductions from total income to arrive at adjusted gross income ("AGI"). Depending on your circumstances, not all deductions are created equal. The adjustments addressed on the first page of Form 1040 (lines 23-37 on the 2016 Form) can be "better" for you than the itemized (Schedule A) or standard deductions claimed on the second page of Form 1040. These deductions include: student loan interest, HSA contribution deduction, moving expenses, IRA contributions, and alimony paid.

Nearly everything that occurs on the second page of Form 1040 is based on your AGI. If AGI is lower it is beneficial for many reasons on the Federal return and, depending on where you live, state income tax purposes. At a certain level of AGI, itemized deductions are capped and eventually phased out. Likewise, most tax credits have an AGI limitation. Thus, adjustments on page 1 of Form 1040 will reduce your AGI which could lead to additional benefits later in the return. Additionally, programs like FAFSA (Federal Student Aid) and other government benefit programs calculate need based on AGI rather than gross income or taxable income.

B. Deductions from Adjusted Gross Income to Arrive at Taxable Income

Deductions from AGI are the more well-known deductions which occur on the second page of Form 1040 after your AGI is calculated. These deductions encompass the personal exemption for you, your spouse, and your children ($4,050 per person in 2016). There is also the proverbial choice between claiming the "Standard Deduction" or the "Itemized Deductions."

The purpose of the Standard and Itemized deductions is to calculate your taxable income. After calculating taxable income, the appropriate rate of tax is applied to that income to calculate your total tax due. The current tax rates (or tax brackets) are: 10%, 15%, 25%, 28%, 33%, 35% and 39.6%, and which bracket you fall in is determined by your filing status. Thus, a Single filing status taxpayer with $100,000 of taxable income for the year will owe $28,000 tax because taxable income of $100,000 is in the 28% bracket.

1. STANDARD DEDUCTIONS

The Standard Deduction, as set forth in the Code, adjusts each year and is based on filing status - Single, Head of Household, Married Filing Separately, Qualifying Widower or Married Filing Jointly. For a single taxpayer in 2016 (whether that means he/she uses the Single or Married Filing Separately status), the standard deduction is $6,300. Double that for a married filing jointly taxpayer or qualifying widower ($12,600). The general rule is to use the Standard Deduction unless the Itemized Deductions will be more than the Standard Deduction. The Standard Deduction is elected by simply checking the box on the side of the second page of the Form 1040. The common standard deductions are: Medical expenses, taxes paid, mortgage interest and points paid, charitable contributions, and job expenses

2. ITEMIZED DEDUCTIONS

Itemized Deductions are claimed on Schedule A, Form 1040. This is the first of many additional forms you can attach to Form 1040. As noted in the discussion on Standard Deductions, you do not choose Itemized Deductions if the Standard Deduction is equal to, or larger than, the sum of your Itemized Deductions. Certain itemized deductions are subject to phase outs if your income is above a certain threshold ($311,300 for a married couple filing jointly). In addition to the phase-out, other restrictions often prevent taxpayers from claiming the full benefit of some itemized deductions. Most restrictive is the 10% of AGI limit for deductible medical expenses. This means that, in 2016 for taxpayers born after January 2, 1952, qualified medical expenses are deductible as itemized deductions to the extent they *exceed* the annual AGI limit. Assume you are a 55 year-old taxpayer with $100,000 of AGI in 2016, and $11,000 of deductible medical expenses during the year. The first $10,000 of your medical expenses are not deductible because of the 10% AGI floor ($100,000 * 10% = $10,000) thus you are only allowed to deduct $1,000 as an itemized deduction.

VI. Tax Credits to Reduce Tax and Arrive at Amount Due or Refund

After calculating the amount of tax due, there is a series of credits you might qualify for that reduce, on a dollar-for-dollar basis, the amount of tax you owe. As with deductions, there are two different sets of credits – nonrefundable and refundable. They are named as such because the nonrefundable credits can reduce the amount of tax you owe to $0, but not below, while refundable credits can increase or create a refund. Credits generally have strict qualification requirements including, among other, an AGI cap.

Common nonrefundable credits include the Education Credits, Child Tax Credit, Foreign Tax Credit and the Credit for Child and Dependent Care Expenses. The common refundable credits are the Earned Income Credit, Additional Child Tax Credit and the American Opportunity Credit. Nonrefundable credits are applied to your tax due first, followed by any tax payments you have made during the year (for example Federal taxes withheld in Box 2 of Form W-2).

After applying nonrefundable credits and payments to reduce the amount of tax due when Form 1040 is filed, the refundable credits are applied to further reduce your tax due and, if you are lucky, produce or increase your already sizable refund.

VII. Dealing with the Internal Revenue Service

One of the most common situations you may encounter that requires a qualified tax attorney is if you receive a notice from the IRS which claims you have underpaid your taxes for a particular year. Depending on the situation, these issues can either be cleared up in a few phone calls or it is the first day on a months-long journey. It goes without saying that the earlier address this issue, including speaking with a qualified tax attorney, the greater your likelihood of success.

Chapter 5: Taxation Attorneys

Throwing IRS notices away, waiting to call your attorney or CPA after the IRS has first garnished your wages, hoping the IRS will forget about you, or ignoring their communications is an extremely inefficient manner of dealing with the IRS.

The IRS is the federal agency charged with enforcing our tax laws. As applied to most taxpayers, the IRS has two primary functions: (1) Examination or Audit and (2) Collection.

A. EXAMINATION OR AUDIT

Examination or audit is the day-to-day function of the IRS. It is how the IRS enforces compliance with the Code. The vast majority of IRS audits today are done by mail rather than sending out an auditor to your home or office. You are notified that the IRS has examined your return and identified a discrepancy when you receive a "CP-2000" notice or "CP75" or "CP75A."

The IRS issues a CP-2000 notice when it identifies additional income you failed to report. For example, a Form 1099-MISC you receive for a side job which you failed to include on your return is reported to the IRS. Generally, you have two choices to respond: (1) agree to the change and pay the excess balance due within 30 days of the notice or (2) disagree with the proposed change by submitting a signed statement disputing the adjustment within 30 days of the notice.

The IRS issues a CP75 notice when it selects your return for audit and want more information. Again, a response within 30 days from the date of the letter is your goal. If you provide the IRS with documentation it will review it and contact you if it needs even more information. After review is complete, the IRS may accept your position, in which case you are finished, or propose an adjustment to your return. If you agree with the IRS' adjustment, you are finished. If you disagree you have several options for appealing the decision. If you can agree to the adjustment during any one of the appeals levels.

If you continue to disagree, or fail to respond within the 30-day period, the IRS will issue a Notice of Deficiency letter or "90-Day Letter." You have similar rights once the Notice of Deficiency is issued as you did during the 30-day period, with a couple of exceptions. You can now file a lawsuit with the U.S. Tax Court or request an audit reconsideration.

B. Collection and Notices

If the 90-day period expires and nothing is done to address the problem, your case moves from Examination to Collections. If you continue to do nothing, the IRS is authorized to garnish wages, seize property, file liens, and levy bank accounts, until the balance due is satisfied. In this situation, you have the following options:

1. Agree with the IRS changes and pay the deficiency. Entering an installment agreement is often beneficial.
2. Request an audit reconsideration if you disagree with the IRS' examination.
3. File an Offer in Compromise.
4. Request a Collection Due Process (CDP) appeal hearing.
5. If you really believe the IRS is wrong on a point of law when analyzing your case, you can pay the deficiency and file a suit for refund in Federal District Court.

Once your case reaches Collections, the issue is rather serious. The IRS does strive to work with you to resolve your accounts without taking more drastic steps. However, the best practice after receiving an IRS notice is to read the notice and understand it. The notices are full of information. If you do not understand it then you should seek the assistance of a qualified tax attorney. Additionally, respond to the notice within the time identified on the notice. If you do these two things, working with the IRS is much easier.

VIII. STATES

States receive most of their revenue – that which is not received from the federal government – from sales taxes and income taxes. There are seven states that impose no income tax on their citizens or residents. Those seven are Florida, Washington, Texas, Nevada, Alaska, Wyoming and South Dakota. Additionally, in New Hampshire and Tennessee, no income tax is imposed on income other than dividends and income from investments. For the rest of us, in the other forty- one states, tax is calculated, assessed, and collected, in a manner similar to the Federal system. A return is prepared based on the income earned or attributed to the state, deductions earned in the state, and tax credits offered by the state. States charge a much lower rate of income tax than the Federal government. However, it is a double taxation system. This means you will pay tax at both Federal and state levels on roughly the same taxable income.

Most states with income taxes incorporate the Code and employ a federal starting point for determining your state taxable income. For example, Missouri uses AGI from your Federal Form 1040 as its starting point while North Dakota and a few others use Federal Taxable Income as their starting point. While this generally makes state taxes for most individuals "easier" to complete, it also emphasizes the importance of preparing your Federal Form 1040 correctly.

ABOUT THE AUTHOR

Zachary Goff
Attorney, Oswald Roam & Rew LLC
www.orrf-law.com
(816) 229-8121

Zachary Goff is an attorney with the Oswald Roam & Rew, LLC, law firm in Blue Springs, Missouri. Zach is a native of Independence, Missouri, who graduated with his B.A. in Political Science from the University of Missouri-Columbia. Zach served four years of active duty in the United States Army as an officer. He achieved the rank of captain before leaving the military to pursue a career in law. He obtained his J.D. from the University of Missouri-Kansas City School of Law where he was a staff member of the UMKC Law Review and Urban Lawyer journals and obtained his LL.M. degree in tax law. After law school, and prior to entering private law practice, Zach worked for several years in a public company's tax research and tax counsel groups. Zach is a member of the Missouri Bar and admitted to practice before the United States Tax Court.

CHAPTER 6:
Criminal Law Attorneys

By: Molly Hastings

"I am so excited to hire a criminal defense attorney to represent me!"

- Said NO ONE EVER

I. Introduction

Most people in the position of needing a criminal defense attorney to represent them are rarely at their best. Being accused of a crime, guilty or not, can be expensive, embarrassing, and potentially life-changing based on the outcome of your case. This chapter is intended to give guidance to those who find themselves being prosecuted for a crime and need to know what to look for in a criminal defense attorney. It will also help you understand what your attorney will expect from you in order to best represent you.

II. 5 Things You Want in a Defense Attorney

A. Fearlessness

A common and not entirely unfounded fear among criminal defendants is that their attorney will deter them from having a jury trial despite the client's desire to have one. Often times, people worry that they will be pressured into a guilty plea against their wishes. Many seasoned criminal defense attorneys can have an extensive legal career and never try a single case in front of a jury. But it is important to know that your lawyer's willingness to try a case can ultimately lead to a better resolution for you in the long run.

The choice to have a trial in a criminal case is entirely up to the defendant. Every defendant has the sole discretion to decide three things during the course of his or her case.

1. Do you want to plead guilty or do you want to have a trial?
2. Do you want to have a jury trial or a bench trial?
3. Do you wish to testify or not during your trial?

An attorney who fails to advise you that these are in fact YOUR rights and your rights alone, is doing you a disservice. It is your attorney's duty to counsel you. This is why attorneys are called "counselors at law". An attorney's obligation to the client is to explain the client's rights, discuss the strengths and weaknesses in the case against him or her, and offer guidance regarding what the attorney believes is best strategy for the client to achieve the most favorable result. Sometimes that is a guilty plea. Sometimes that is a jury trial. The best outcome is when both the attorney and the client agree on the most effective strategy to resolve a case and protect the client. However, if you and your attorney disagree as to whether your case should and will be brought to trial, the decision ultimately rests with you. A good defense attorney is willing to respect your decision and honor your wishes to proceed to trial, even if it is against his or her advice. Before you hire anyone to represent you, clarify with that attorney "if I want a trial, will you agree to try my case, no matter what?" If the answer is anything short of "ABSOLUTELY", keep looking until you find the fearless attorney you need.

B. Transparency

People in need of a criminal defense attorney are often in desperate situations. As a result, they are eager for any good news regarding their case or what the outcome will be. Understandably, it is difficult as an attorney to deliver bad news to a hopeful client. But be wary of the lawyer who only reports positive feedback and optimistic predictions. Your lawyer has an obligation to educate you about the investigation and weight of the evidence against you, the laws that apply, and the risk involved in taking your case to trial. Your attorney is also required to fully explain any and all plea offers extended during the course of your case. If a client tells me at the inception of his or her case that he or she is completely uninterested in a plea offer and will only be satisfied with a trial, I know that it is still my duty to make my client aware of any and all plea offers extended to him or her, even if I know that offer will be rejected. Having a frank conversation with a client about the challenges he or she faces based on the evidence against him or her or the likelihood of an inevitable prison sentence is never something an attorney looks forward to. But failing to have the conversation to save both the attorney and client from the discomfort of discussing difficult issues does a disservice to everyone. You need a lawyer who will give you the good news with the bad so you can make the best decision for yourself on how to proceed with your case.

C. Availability

One of the most frequent complaints lodged against attorneys when being reported to the bar is a refusal to communicate with the client. You deserve a lawyer who will call you back. It's that simple. Requiring your attorney to return your call is not too much to ask. If people get busy, it's understandable. We are all busy. It's part of being a productive adult. But if you cannot reach your attorney after a reasonable amount of time, you should look for a different lawyer. Now, this is not to say that bombarding your attorney with relentless phone calls and emails on a daily basis is appropriate either. Respecting each other's time and effort is key to effective communication. But if your attempts to contact your attorney have fallen on deaf ears, find a new lawyer. Communication between a client and his or her attorney is essential to the client's representation. You deserve a lawyer who will fully engage in that communication. No one is too busy to return a phone call if he or she is committed to working for you.

D. Reputation in the Legal Community

Research the attorney you consider hiring. Verify the results the attorney achieved in previous cases. Find out what other attorneys think of your potential attorney. Ensure the attorney is in good standing with the bar by contacting your local bar association. Read the reviews and testimonials from past clients who have used the attorney's services. An attorney who is respected by clients and colleagues alike is an obvious asset to your defense. If your attorney has a strong working relationship with opposing counsel, this does not mean that you are at a disadvantage because he or she appears to "get along with" the prosecutor in your case. There is a misconception that if your lawyer is friendly or amicable with the prosecuting attorney, this must mean that he or she is not effectively fighting for you. The expectation that all attorney negotiations and contact must be contentious and combative in order for a client to be best represented is unreasonable. Successful attorneys can be adversaries of one another without necessarily being enemies. It is to your benefit to have an attorney who is respected among the defense bar as well as those on the prosecution's side.

E. No Promised Results

It is tempting to hire the first attorney to assure you that he or she: (a) can get your case dismissed, (b) can guarantee that you will avoid incarceration, or (c) can and will win your case at trial, etc. There is nothing wrong with an attorney who is confident in his or her skills and talents. There is something wrong however with an attorney who promises you an absolute result. Be leery when you are told at your first consultation with a prospective attorney that for the right price, he or she can promise that you get the exact result you want. This is an unenforceable promise. And frankly, it is an incredibly reckless way to practice law.

Each case is different. Each case comes with its own set of circumstances and facts, its own prosecutor and judge, and obviously each defendant in each case brings a different set of factors to the table. There is no formula to any case that can produce an absolute outcome, despite what an attorney may guarantee. The only promise that any attorney should make to you in attempting to gain your business and your trust, is the promise to work hard and get you the best possible result he or she can.

Clients often ask attorneys to predict the likelihood of a case being dismissed or winning at trial. Attorneys should always decline to answer this question. If the prediction is wrong, the attorney has done nothing but give you false hope of a result that he or she could not deliver. If you consider hiring a lawyer that is unabashedly promising you that you have a 100% chance of winning your case so long as you hire him or her, don't take the bait. No one can or should promise you a result. So, be mindful of this in choosing your attorney. There is no benefit to paying someone to simply tell you what you desperately want to hear.

III. 5 Things Your Defense Attorney Wants from You, the Defendant

A. Money

There is some truth to all the greedy lawyer jokes out there! But we all must make a living. Even your lawyer. No one ever wants to hire a criminal defense attorney. The cost is often unexpected and the need is almost always immediate. Representing yourself in a criminal case is never advised. But your lawyer needs to get paid. Using the services of your attorney is just like using the services of any professional. You want your kitchen sink repaired? You hire a plumber and pay to have it fixed. You want representation in court? You must hire a lawyer and pay your bill. Be prepared to ask your attorney his or her fee in advance, work out how expenses will be covered, if and what kind of payment plan is acceptable, what kind of additional costs to expect, etc. If both parties have a clear understanding of the financial expectations on the front end of the representation, it makes for a much smoother relationship. You want an attorney to spend his or her time working on your defense, not spending that time as a bill collector chasing you for money. If you enter into an agreement with your attorney to pay a designated amount for his or her services, honor that agreement. It's how business works. Nothing will ruin a client-attorney relationship faster than a client who refuses to make a good faith effort to pay for an attorney's services, despite having previously agreed to do just that.

B. Accessibility

Often, in a criminal case, plea offers are extended at the last minute, on the eve of trial, with a deadline by which time they need to be accepted or the plea offer will be revoked. It is also not uncommon for a court date to change unexpectedly and immediate notification is necessary. It is incredibly important that your lawyer can reach you in these circumstances. If your attorney is unable to contact you, you run the risk of a warrant being issued for your arrest, losing the chance to accept a good plea offer, or generally being unaware of updates on your case as they happen. Advise your attorney at your first meeting how best to contact you, whether that be through email, text, phone call, etc. Make sure your attorney has updated information at all times. You have one lawyer. Your lawyer however may have dozens and dozens of clients. It is your responsibility to inform your attorney of changes of address or phone number so that he or she can focus on working on your defense, not tracking you down when it's time to relay important information. It is an incredibly difficult task to represent people who are unengaged or uninterested in the status and progress of their pending case. You will be a more satisfied and better informed client if you actively participate in communicating with your attorney and making yourself available to him or her through regularly updated contact information.

As stated earlier, you want your attorney to be accessible. And your attorney wants the same out of you.

C. Patience

No criminal case is ever resolved as quickly as anyone wants. It is not uncommon to see a misdemeanor takes six months or more to resolve favorably for a client and felonies rarely get to trial in under a year's time. Your willingness to allow your case to take its course will also allow your attorney the time he or she needs to get you the best possible result. This is a lot to ask, as most defendants are anxious to put their case behind them and forget they were ever in the position of being charged with a crime in the first place. But getting the quickest result and getting the right result are not always the same thing.

Your behavior and actions while a case is pending against you are crucial to the final outcome. The time between when charges are brought against you and the final disposition of the case is probably the most scrutinized time period of all by judges and prosecutors alike. Make the most of it. This is an opportunity for you to show that you are capable of and willing to be a law abiding and productive citizen. It is your chance to prove that the charges filed against you are the exception to how you ordinarily live your day to day life. Use this time wisely to maintain employment, complete drug or alcohol treatment, make efforts towards restitution, seek mental health counseling, or actively participate in community service and activities. These things can serve as mitigation for your charges and may influence the ultimate outcome of your case. The time it takes for a case to take its course can often serve to help you in distancing yourself from the charges you face and the acts that have been alleged.

D. Cooperation

Cooperation is not the same as blind compliance. Your attorney expects you to have meaningful questions and concerns about the progress of your case. Ask them. You have a right to be fully informed of your situation so you can make the best choices for yourself in this process. Cooperation simply means to keep the easy stuff easy. Show up for all your court dates. Make sure your attorney can reach you. Read your discovery. Provide your lawyer with witness information. Make your appointments. Don't break the law! Seems simple enough, and it makes an incredible difference to your attorney's ability to do the best job he or she can for you as your advocate. If your attorney advises you that there is a specific goal you can work toward while your case is pending, listen to him or her. Make every effort to follow through. It may ultimately impact the result of your case in a way that benefits you. If attending drug treatment or anger management improves your chances of getting a favorable result, listen to your lawyer and work with him or her to get this done. Your cooperation with your lawyer's directives can translate into your willingness to cooperate with a probation officer, and can often be used as mitigation to get you a plea offer that avoids incarceration altogether. Again, your lawyer should not promise you a result. But if your attorney gives you guidance as to certain actions you can take to improve your circumstances, your cooperation can make all the difference.

E. No Surprises

There are few feelings worse for a defense attorney than thinking you are completely prepared and fully informed about a case, and then being blind-sided in court by a prosecutor with information that has a terribly negative impact on your defense. Defendants will occasionally fail to provide all the necessary information to their attorneys out of embarrassment or shame, or in effort to make their situation appear better than it is. Though this strategy may appear to be helpful in terms of saving face or self-preservation, it puts your attorney at a real disadvantage.

Your attorney is much like your doctor in a lot of ways. First and foremost, your conversations with either are confidential and privileged. Second, much like your doctor, your attorney has seen it all. An experienced attorney is rarely shocked by any information divulged by a client. Do not be ashamed or embarrassed. It serves you well to be honest and forthcoming with your lawyer so he or she is adequately prepared to deal with bad evidence. It is a much softer blow to learn about unfavorable information directly from a client during private conversations, than to find out in court from a prosecutor or in discovery from law enforcement. If your lawyer knows the full picture, then your lawyer can best defend against it. A doctor can give you a more accurate diagnosis if you tell him or her about all of your symptoms. A defense attorney can better defend you if you inform him or her of all the important facts of your case, even the incriminating stuff. YOUR CONVERSATIONS WITH YOUR ATTORNEY ARE CONFIDENTIAL. Whatever you share with your attorney can never be used against you. You are not protecting yourself by failing to disclose information to your attorney, no matter how unfavorable. It is your attorney's job to protect you and defend you against all accusations, and your attorney is most effective when he or she is provided with the most information you can give to him or her.

IV. Conclusion

In conclusion, hiring a criminal defense attorney is an unwanted and uncomfortable necessity when you find yourself charged with a crime. But, taking the time to ask the right questions and vet the right lawyer is worth it to you in the long run. There are few situations in life that are more serious than the risk of losing your freedom. Before hiring anyone, make sure your attorney appreciates the gravity your situation presents. Your rights deserve to be protected. You are entitled to a vigorous defense. And you should never settle for less than a zealous and committed advocate.

ABOUT THE AUTHOR

Molly M. Hastings
Managing Attorney,
The Hastings Law Firm
www.hastingslawfirmonline.com
Tel: (816) 423-2530

Since 2001, **Molly Hastings** has focused her entire career on criminal defense and trial practice. After 13 years as a dedicated public defender in both rural and urban jurisdictions, Molly transitioned into private practice. She has tried over 50 felony jury trials, with incredible success, including acquittals for 1st degree and 2nd degree murder, forcible rape, child molestation, first degree assault, and involuntary manslaughter. Molly was awarded the Charles M. Shaw Award for Excellence in Trial Advocacy in 2009 and the Lon O. Hocker Award in 2013. Molly is regularly featured on both local and national television for defending some of Kansas City's most serious cases.

CHAPTER 7:
Bankruptcy Attorneys

By: Jeffrey L. Wagoner

I. Introduction

There are many factors to consider when hiring a bankruptcy attorney. In no particular order, you should consider:

1. The attorney's experience level;
2. Where the attorney is in the life cycle of his practice;
3. What size of firm will work best for your particular case;
4. The attorney's support staff;
5. How was initial contact with the firm;
6. What is the attorney's mindset;
7. How much are the fees quoted and more importantly, what are the details;
8. How did the initial consultation go;
9. How will the preparation of the petition, schedules and other documents be handled; and
10. How did you find the attorney and what clues does the internet hold about the attorney?

Keep in mind that the type of bankruptcy help you need may very well dictate which attorney is best for you. For example, my firm's strength is in consumer Chapter 7 and Chapter 13 cases. I always refer potential Chapter 11 and Chapter 12 cases to other law firms – we just are not set up to handle those types of cases. Which attorney is best for your situation will depend on whether it's a consumer bankruptcy, or a very small business that has failed, or a medium sized enterprise in trouble. Or, maybe you are a creditor and need help protecting or asserting your rights in someone else's bankruptcy. The vast majority of people who seek assistance in bankruptcy need a consumer Chapter 7 or Chapter 13 bankruptcy. Those cases make up about 99% of cases filed across the United States. This chapter mainly focuses on those cases. However, many people have small businesses in trouble and others need assistance protecting their rights as a creditor, so we'll discuss those as well.

II. Experience as an Attorney

The first two questions to ask when hiring a bankruptcy attorney is: (1) How many years has the attorney practiced overall? and (2) What year was he or she first licensed to practice law? This doesn't mean that a new attorney can't do a good job. But, it sure makes it harder without experience. Many lessons are learned after law school in the school of hard knocks. Unlike doctors, attorneys don't have a residency or internship requirement. After completing 6 semesters of law school, a graduate is ready to tackle the bar exam for his or her respective state. It is important to understand that the bar exam is a test to ensure minimum competency in the understanding of law, not mastery of the law or how to handle a case for a client. In a nutshell, the bar exam is nothing more than one more test covering all of the subjects that the fresh law school graduate should have studied in law school. The bar exam is not administered by a law school – it is done by the state bar association, with oversight by the state's supreme court. The purpose of the bar exam is to ensure the potential new attorney understands the basics of the state's law in each of many different areas of the law.

Chapter 7: Bankruptcy Attorneys

Once the fresh law school graduate successfully passes the bar exam, he or she is required to take an oath of office as an officer of the court. After that, as well as passing a background check, he or she is then licensed as a bright, shiny new attorney. It is a great accomplishment, for certain. But, most new attorneys have very little experience actually practicing law. And then there's the matter of successfully operating a law firm. A law firm is no different than any other business – if it is not done well, the firm will fail and the firm's clients will suffer. If you decide to hire an attorney with less than 5 years' experience, consider asking whether that attorney works for, or at least is mentored by, a more experienced attorney.

The next factor to consider is the number of years the attorney has spent practicing bankruptcy law. Bankruptcy law comes generally from 4 sources: (1) the Federal Bankruptcy Code, (2) the Bankruptcy Rules of Procedure, (3) Case Law, and (4) what I like to call "the unwritten rules." The Bankruptcy Code establishes the types of bankruptcy (Chapter 7, Chapter 9, Chapter 11, Chapter 12, Chapter 13 and Chapter 15). It establishes the substance of how bankruptcy works. The Bankruptcy Rules of Procedure deal with how the bankruptcy court runs its cases. Both of these sets of laws are extremely complex and take years to fully understand. Here's just one subsection of one provision of the Bankruptcy Code (11 USC § 541):

> (a) The commencement of a case under section 301, 302, or 303 of this title creates an estate. Such estate is comprised of all the following property, wherever located and by whomever held:
>
>> (1) Except as provided in subsections (b) and (c)(2) of this section, all legal or equitable interests of the debtor in property as of the commencement of the case.
>>
>> (2) All interests of the debtor and the debtor's spouse in community property as of the commencement of the case that is—
>>
>>> (A) under the sole, equal, or joint management and control of the debtor; or

(B) liable for an allowable claim against the debtor, or for both an allowable claim against the debtor and an allowable claim against the debtor's spouse, to the extent that such interest is so liable.

(3) Any interest in property that the trustee recovers under section 329(b), 363(n), 543, 550, 553, or 723 of this title.

(4) Any interest in property preserved for the benefit of or ordered transferred to the estate under section 510(c) or 551 of this title.

(5) Any interest in property that would have been property of the estate if such interest had been an interest of the debtor on the date of the filing of the petition, and that the debtor acquires or becomes entitled to acquire within 180 days after such date—

(A) by bequest, devise, or inheritance;

(B) as a result of a property settlement agreement with the debtor's spouse, or of an interlocutory or final divorce decree; or

(C) as a beneficiary of a life insurance policy or of a death benefit plan.

You can see how the Bankruptcy Code cross references other code sections at seemingly every opportunity. It's as if the people who wrote the Bankruptcy Code are all in on one big inside joke – subsection (a)(3) alone has *SIX* references to other code sections, and that's all contained in one sentence. You don't gain a good understanding of the law governing bankruptcy until you've worked with it for several years.

"The Unwritten Rules," are even trickier. Every jurisdiction has its own quirks and idiosyncrasies. These are things as simple as how much property a trustee wants to have available before the trustee will consider opening a bankruptcy estate (which is described above in the excerpt from Section 541). They can be as complicated as the local

U.S. Trustee's office's policies on certain Means Test criteria. There are a lot of these rules and they aren't written down anywhere. You learn them from familiarity with the local bankruptcy practice. And that comes only with time spent in the local bankruptcy trenches.

All of the above information applies to any bankruptcy lawyer. But, the type of bankruptcy assistance you need will determine the attorney you should hire. If you are looking for help protecting and enforcing your rights as a creditor, then a firm that represents consumer debtors (such as my firm) probably isn't your best bet. You probably want to find a law firm that specializes in representing creditors. A firm that specializes in creditor work would be a poor choice to file a consumer Chapter 7 or Chapter 13 case. Some bankruptcy attorneys act mainly as trustees, which are sort of "referees" to administer bankruptcy cases and recover assets for the benefit of creditors. Typically, bankruptcy attorneys who do a lot of trustee work also make very good attorneys to help creditors protect their rights. Some attorneys who act as trustees also are excellent at representing consumer Chapter 7 and Chapter 13 debtors. However, it is rare to see an attorney who acts as a trustee also do both creditor work and represent consumer Chapter 7 and Chapter 13 cases. Although all bankruptcy attorneys are working with the same set of laws and judges, the skillset required for the different roles (creditor, trustee, business debtor, consumer debtor) are vastly different.

Specifically, when hiring a consumer debtor's attorney to file a Chapter 7 or Chapter 13 case, you should also consider the size of the law firm the attorney has practiced in and gotten most of his or her experience with. Big law firms (i.e., 100 attorneys or more) typically hire the top law school graduates. The big law firms have starting salaries to attract the best talent coming out of law school. However, the big law firms don't keep every new lawyer that they hire straight out of law school. Some of those very bright young attorneys find themselves starting their own practices after several years spent working at a big law firm. Although he or she is very bright, that experience at a big law firm does not prepare an attorney to handle a consumer bankruptcy. Those fresh-from-the-big-firms attorneys have little experience working with the extremely limited resources that a

Chapter 7 or Chapter 13 case has to pay attorney fees. The former big firm attorney generally doesn't have much face-to-face contact with clients and likely had absolutely zero contact with a consumer client while at the big law firm. They need time in a consumer practice to get their bearings and understand how best to serve this new-to-them type of client.

Becoming a good bankruptcy practitioner requires experience working in the trenches. I you are looking for an attorney to file a consumer Chapter 7 or Chapter 13 case, ask how many cases the attorney has previously filed. If the attorney has not personally filed at least 500 cases, then that attorney is still learning the ropes. However, if you are a business looking to hire an attorney to file a Chapter 11 case, understand that there simply aren't that many Chapter 11 cases filed each year. Experience in 15 different Chapter 11 cases would indicate a decent level of experience for a Chapter 11 attorney.

III. WHERE IS THE ATTORNEY IN THE LIFECYCLE OF HIS OR HER PRACTICE?

Based on the above, you might think the best bet is to hire the oldest, most experienced attorney you can find. But, that's not always the best option. What if the attorney you are hiring is getting ready to retire? That might mean he's already got one foot out the door and maybe isn't that motivated to do a great job for you. What happens if an issue arises with your case a couple of years from now, when you thought your case was finished, and your attorney closed up shop and retired to Florida? What if the older attorney begins to have health issues and is unable to maintain his law practice?

Is the attorney you are considering in the midst of building a new practice? If so, he or she may be motivated to work extra hard on your case. The lack of experience may be made up, at least partly, by the willingness to go the extra mile. The attorney building a new practice knows that a happy client is the most effective and least expensive kind of advertising. On the other hand, understand that growing a new practice area requires creating the infrastructure to effectively serve those new clients. There are growing pains in establishing a new practice area even if the lawyer is overall very experienced.

Another question to ask is: "What led you to practice this type of law?" The practice of law is mentally very grueling. Attorneys wake up every morning and head into the office knowing full well they will be saddled with everyone else's problems that day. Day after day, year after year doing nothing but dealing with crisis after crisis. Look for signs of burnout in any attorney you consider hiring. For consumer Chapter 7 and Chapter 13 cases, if the attorney you hire got into bankruptcy just to pay the bills, that's a big red flag because, simply put, there isn't a lot of profit in serving consumer bankruptcy clients. The attorney might be frustrated at how difficult it is to make a decent living as a consumer bankruptcy attorney. Consequently, there is a significant public service component to consumer bankruptcy practice – if the attorney doesn't enjoy helping people through a very difficult time in their lives and doesn't take a great deal of satisfaction in the non-monetary benefits of a bankruptcy practice, then that attorney probably won't be happy practicing this type of law. Look for an attorney who has a passion for consumer bankruptcy law if you are filing a Chapter 7 or Chapter 13 case.

IV. MULTI-LAWYER SMALL FIRM OF VARIOUS DISCIPLINES VS. SOLO PRACTITIONER VS. BOUTIQUE FIRM VS. BIG FIRM

As mentioned above, the practice of law is very different between big firms (100 or more attorneys) and small firms (10 or fewer attorneys). Big firm attorneys typically practice in a very specific niche of the law and don't need to worry about the day-to-day details of running a law firm such as dealing with a copier that has just broken down (big firms have people to handle that). If you are a medium size or bigger company and you need to file a Chapter 11 bankruptcy, you'll probably need several attorneys working together who specialize in Chapter 11 work. Most likely, a big law firm will be well equipped to properly handle a major Chapter 11 bankruptcy case.

Consumer bankruptcy cases are often handled by solo practitioners or firms made up of only two attorneys. They do this type of work quite well. You simply don't need a large law firm to handle those types of cases. Likewise, some small firms of 4 to 10 attorneys may have only one bankruptcy attorney in the firm. Each attorney in that firm may specialize in a different area of the law. This is typically an effective way to build a firm as the lawyers can refer work to one another. The problem comes when you hire that firm to handle your bankruptcy and then the one bankruptcy attorney in the firm is not available to deal with a problem that arises in your case because he or she is on vacation or out sick or just busy with another case. Ask the question "Who else does this firm have available to assist me if you are out of the office?" They may very well have an arrangement with another small firm to step in to cover cases when one attorney is out, but it is an important point.

A "boutique firm" is a small firm that specializes in one area of the law. Think of a boutique firm as being a group of attorneys that would work together in just one practice area in a big firm. A big firm's bankruptcy department might consist of five bankruptcy attorneys, for example. Boutique firms are sometimes created when a department of a big firm breaks away from the big firm to start its own firm. A boutique firm may be a good choice for a medium sized company seeking to file a Chapter 11 bankruptcy because the firm has all of the expertise and firepower of a big firm, but without the cumbersome and expensive bureaucracy that comes with those big firms. Therefore, the boutique firm may be able to react quicker and charge less than the bankruptcy department of a big firm. Boutique firms also serve consumer bankruptcy clients. These consumer boutique firms have everyone in the firm focused on one type of law. They have procedures and processes for effectively managing a very large caseload because this is the only type of work that they do. A consumer boutique firm enjoys the economy of scale over solo practitioners and two attorney shops – the overhead of running a law firm can be shared among 5 to 10 attorneys rather than being borne by one or two attorneys. The attorneys in a boutique firm can also consult with their colleagues in the firm on tough issues that may arise. In the boutique law firm, since every attorney is basically practicing the same type of law, having one or two attorneys unavailable won't significantly impact the firm's ability to service its clients.

No matter what size firm you hire, be absolutely certain that there is at least one other attorney who is ready, willing, and able to step in to assist if the primary attorney is unavailable.

V. STAFF

A good attorney needs good staff to assist with the day-to-day business of running a law practice. Experienced paralegals make a tremendous difference in effectively serving clients and managing a caseload. Just as there is a concern for any practice that relies on one attorney, you should be concerned if the attorney you hire has only one staff member to assist that attorney. I would look for multiple staff members involved in the bankruptcy practice for the firm you hire. Typically, one paralegal will be the lead staff person, but that person will have one or more assistants to handle the caseload. You should ask questions to see who the bankruptcy paralegals and legal assistants are in the firm because, chances are, a great deal of the work done on your case will be done by these people.

The helpfulness of these same staff members becomes an important factor in evaluating who to hire. Do the staff members willingly help the firm's clients in addressing routine issues? Are they friendly? Do they seem knowledgeable and experienced?

VI. INITIAL CONTACT WITH FIRM

First impressions are extremely important and the law firm you hire should make the effort to create a good one. Consumers typically visit a firm's website before ever contacting the law firm for a first consultation. Did that law firm's website give you the impression that the firm has the expertise to assist you? Or, does the firm's website look like a canned website that was simply created from a template?

When you made that first call to set an initial consultation appointment, who answered your call? Was it the attorney himself or herself? While it's nice to speak directly to the attorney, be a little skeptical as to why the attorney is answering the phone. It may be necessary for attorneys to answer the firm phone on occasion. But, if your attorney answers the phone on a regular basis, it may be a sign that he or she probably doesn't have an adequate support staff.

Did you send an e-mail to the attorney after the initial consultation? If yes, how long did it take him or her to answer the email? If you want an immediate answer to a question, you should call the office and speak to the staff, who will either answer the question or find an attorney who can. But, if you choose to email, your attorney should respond to that email within 24 hours as a general rule. A good attorney will set an automatic reply to emails telling the sender that he or she is out of the office, who to contact during the absence, and when he or she expects to be back in the office.

A couple of more signs of a well-run bankruptcy practice, especially for the consumer bankruptcy case, is whether you receive a reminder call before your initial consultation with your attorney and also whether the firm followed up after initial consult.

VII. Attorney Mindset

An important factor in your bankruptcy case and the overall experience you have is the attorney's mindset. Is the attorney friendly? If not, that may signal burnout or a general malaise in the firm's practice. Is the attorney overly cautious? There are issues and potential problems in almost every bankruptcy case, but a good attorney can adapt and work around those issues. While there are no guarantees that a case will go smoothly, sometimes the best option to help a client with financial difficulties is a bankruptcy, even if that bankruptcy has some "warts". Your attorney shouldn't be afraid to tackle a difficult case – unwillingness to do so may be an indication that the attorney is insecure in his or her abilities or lacks the experience to handle a difficult case.

Likewise, be wary if the attorney is flippant about your case. While an experienced attorney will recognize a simple bankruptcy case and can reassure you that it's a piece of cake, sometimes inexperienced attorneys will simply fail to recognize major issues. If you are like most consumers, you will have done a little research online when contemplating bankruptcy. If you know that there are potential problems in your case, be certain to draw those to the attorney's attention and watch closely how the attorney works through the analysis of that problem. If he or she glosses over the problem, it may be a sign that he or she doesn't understand the problem.

Is the attorney optimistic about your cases' prospects for successful completion? If not, the attorney may be trying to push you out the door. Or, the attorney may see nothing but problems with your case or simply not know how to effectively deal with problems in bankruptcy. If the attorney is not optimistic about getting your case successfully completed, then move along and interview another candidate.

Attorneys, especially experienced attorneys, can become inflexible. But, bankruptcy cases can be very different and not all clients have the same needs. Some clients just want the basics while others need to have their hands held the entire way. Your case may be a routine case, but you might have some special concerns or needs. An attorney needs to be flexible when working with clients. Attorneys should try to say "Yes" to your requests. After all, you are the boss - it's your case and the attorney works for you.

VIII. Fees

Oh boy, here's a factor that is rarely overlooked. In fact, consumer debtors, they use cost as the primary factor in hiring a bankruptcy attorney. After all, they are struggling with their finances, so money is front of mind in most of their decision making. However, cost shouldn't be the primary factor to consider when hiring an attorney. First and foremost, anyone looking to file a bankruptcy should understand that the bankruptcy court limits the fees a firm can charge. If you have a consumer case, many bankruptcy courts set a "no look fee" for routine consumer cases. For example, in the Western District of Missouri in 2017, a bankruptcy attorney can only charge a client up to $3,600 (or $4,100 if the debtor is an "above-median" income earner) without having to submit detailed time and billing records to get approval of his or her fees. Any fees in excess of that amount must be approved by the bankruptcy court after a fee application is filed by the debtor's attorney. So, rarely is any client in bankruptcy going to get taken to the cleaners by a bankruptcy attorney – it just doesn't work that way.

Rather than worrying about being overcharged, beware the low price offers for bankruptcy assistance you may see on Craigslist or elsewhere. Ask about potential add-ons to the advertised fees: are they expected or do they only apply in unusual circumstances? In our market a few years ago, we had several consumer bankruptcy attorneys advertising very low fees in the local shopper newspapers and online. However, they would routinely add on fee after fee for routine services that are required in the normal course of representation of a debtor in a consumer case. The local bankruptcy court created special procedures to guard against those "bait and switch" tactics. In general, you should hire the best bankruptcy attorney that you can and make the fees a secondary factor. Because the bankruptcy court monitors attorney fees, all consumer bankruptcy attorneys charge roughly the same amount.

You should ask any attorney you are considering whether they have payment plans for their fees. If your bankruptcy attorney insists on payment of 100% of his or her fees upfront, then you should shop around. Your bankruptcy attorney should understand that you have limited financial resources and the firm needs to make bankruptcy assistance affordable.

Ask if there will be a written contract or engagement letter detailing the expected fees and potential extra charges. Every decent attorney will insist on a written fee agreement with every client he or she serves. A written agreement provides protection to the client. And, it's an important part of protecting the firm. Good law practice management simply demands written agreements.

IX. INITIAL CONSULT

When hiring a bankruptcy attorney, whether for a consumer case, a business case, or as a creditor representative, you will likely have an initial consultation with the attorney. The attorney is sizing you up as a client just as much as you are sizing up the attorney for whether you'll hire him or her. Is that initial consultation provided free of charge or was there a cost? In our market, almost everyone offers a free consultation for consumer cases. Some attorneys charge for initial consults. Those that do charge either are so good and are so busy that they don't really need new clients or they are unfamiliar with the local market. Either way, it's not a good sign.

When you had the initial consultation, did you meet with a paralegal or with an actual attorney? What was the analysis of your case? Was it an attorney that did the analysis? Do you feel that the law firm took the time to properly review your situation and give you a recommendation? If you didn't get to spend time with and ask questions of an attorney, you probably won't get much time at all with an attorney during your case.

What information were you asked for in your initial consultation? In order to analyze a case, an attorney will need to know quite a bit of information about your assets and debts and your income and expenses. Without that information, it is impossible to accurately advise a potential client on the course of action to take and the potential problems in a case.

How organized was the initial consultation? Did it seem like the firm knew exactly what it was doing during your initial consultation? Was the entire process, from taking your initial call to greeting you upon arrival at the firm to the meeting with attorney and/or staff organized and efficient? Consumer bankruptcy firms, in particular, must be efficient and organized due to the nature of the practice and the limited resources available to pay for attorney fees.

How were the initial consultation documents? Did the firm have its own set of handouts and informational flyers to help you understand the process? Or, did it appear that the firm had very little prepared information or that the information was generic and likely came along with the bankruptcy preparation software program that the firm uses?

How well did the firm educate you as a debtor on the bankruptcy process? Did you feel you understood the bankruptcy process (where you have to go, what you have to do, how long it will take, what it will cost, what are the downsides and what are the risks)?

What was the attorney's recommendation for your case? Was it for a Chapter 7? Or Chapter 13? And WHY did the attorney recommend one bankruptcy chapter over the other? Are there other non-bankruptcy options that the attorney thinks you might wish to consider?

What did the attorney's desk look like? Was it organized? Was there a big pile of work sitting there, indicating that the attorney might have a difficult time managing his or her caseload? Were there files from other clients laying around where you could see names or details about cases? If so, are you comfortable with the thought that your case file might be left out where some other client or potential client might see it?

Look to see if the "law firm" you are visiting is actually simply an office-sharing situation. I have seen many solo practitioners advertise their practice as "Smith and Associates" when in actuality it is a one-attorney shop – there are no "Associates". You need to know if that is the case. Also, is the law office appropriately outfitted? Do they have the equipment and staff to effectively run a law practice?

Finally, when it comes to initial consultations, don't be afraid to get more than one. Generally, initial consultations are free, so the only cost is your time. Competition is a good thing and don't limit yourself to the first attorney you meet.

X. DOCUMENT PREPARATION

In any bankruptcy case, there are going to be A LOT of documents prepared at the very start of the case. Does the attorney hand you a big stack of blank worksheets and expect you to fill them out? The bankruptcy preparation software companies supply a standard set of forms and advise attorneys to force their clients to fill those out. This is a major obstacle for most clients. Working through all of the document preparation together with clients helps the attorney get to know their case, and also know that the document preparation is done correctly. Be wary if your attorney hands you a bunch of forms and expects you to spend hours filling them out.

Ask, at the initial consultation, how much time you will get to spend with the attorney. If you see the attorney for only a few minutes at the initial consultation, expect to spend very little time with him or her when preparing the paperwork.

Ask at the initial consultation if you will receive a copy of all documents that you sign. You should receive a full set of all documents that were filed with the court.

XI. How did you Find the Attorney?

Lastly, when hiring a bankruptcy attorney, consider how you found that attorney. Nowadays, Google is the major source of leads for our practice. But, a close second is a referral by another attorney or a former client. Attorneys love to get referrals, and you should love it if someone will give you a referral. Bankruptcy is a very personal and private thing. It is tough to ask for a bankruptcy attorney recommendation. However, understand that many people go through bankruptcy. Statistics show that half of all divorces lead to one or both parties filing a bankruptcy within 2 years. We all know many people who have suffered through a divorce – did you realize that half of those people have also filed bankruptcy? A referral is a great way to find a good bankruptcy attorney.

If you found your potential bankruptcy attorney through an advertisement, look to see what other services he or she advertises. If the attorney handles 4 or 5 different practices areas (divorce, DUI's, personal injury, contracts, litigation), then be afraid. Be very afraid. You simply cannot be a top notch bankruptcy attorney and practice in multiple disciplines. Some bankruptcy attorneys will successfully practice one other area of law, but handling multiple practices at once simply will not allow you to know the nuances and keep abreast of the frequent changes in bankruptcy.

Go out and look for other online references to any attorney you consider. Just like a company checking out a potential new employee, take the time to do an internet search. While it is normal to have some negative information out there if you have been practicing for years and have served hundreds of clients, you should look for patterns of problems in your online search. Don't be afraid to check with your state's bar association to ask if the attorney has ever been suspended from the practice of law or censored by the state's disciplinary office.

XII. Conclusion

In a nutshell, look for an attorney that not only has practiced for several years, but also one that has several years' experience practicing the type of bankruptcy law for which you need help. As a debtor, don't make price the primary factor in your hiring decision, especially since the bankruptcy court has oversight on fees you will be charged. Ironically, a "cheap" bankruptcy attorney may charge you more in the end. When you hire a bankruptcy attorney, you shouldn't be hiring just one person. You need to know what that attorney's support structure is in terms of staff and a backup attorney.

ABOUT THE AUTHOR

Jeffrey L. Wagoner
President, WM Law
www.kansascitybankruptcy.com
Tel: (913) 422-0909

Jeffrey L. Wagoner is president of Wagoner Bankruptcy Group, P.C. dba WM Law, a fifteen-person firm that represents hundreds of clients yearly in consumer bankruptcy filings in Kansas and Missouri with offices in Kansas City and Independence, Missouri and Olathe, Kansas. He was selected as Best of the Bar for bankruptcy attorneys by the Kansas City Business Journal in 2002, 2003 and 2004. The Kansas City Metropolitan Bar Association's 1997 Young Lawyer of the Year recipient received his Juris Doctor from the University of Missouri-Kansas City in 1995 where he was Technical Editor for the UMKC Law Review. He received his undergraduate degree with honors in 1986 from the University of Missouri-Columbia. Mr. Wagoner is also a decorated veteran of the Operation Desert Storm, serving on active duty flying the S-3 Viking and later as the Commanding Officer of three Navy Reserve units. He retired in 2009 at the rank of Captain. Mr. Wagoner has authored published articles on commercial law, business law and legal procedure.

CHAPTER 8:
Insurance Dispute Attorneys

By: José M. Bautista

I. Introduction: The History of Bad Faith Litigation

Bad faith generally implies that there is malice, ill will, fraud, wrongful intention or a mixture of all the above. Missouri courts define bad faith as a "state of mind" which is shown through the insurance company's acts and the circumstances surrounding the matter.

At one point, insurance claims were fairly predictable. However, bad faith litigation is now a common occurrence throughout the United States and is evolving every day. You may be asking yourself, "How does bad faith work its way into a claim against a motor vehicle insurance company?" Within each contract signed between two parties, there is an implied covenant of good faith and fair dealing. This means that when an insurance policy holder ("Insured" or "You") signs a contract for a motor vehicle policy with an insurance company ("Insurer") there is an implied covenant of good faith and fair dealing that You will not make claims to recoup money from the policy that You do not deserve and that the Insurer will not delay or intentionally deny a claim for no good reason. Essentially, the implied covenant is nothing more than a "Play nice!" that you used to hear when you were a kid.

Bad faith litigation goes beyond recovering damages for someone who was wronged by another but also plays an important in promoting consumer protection and confidence within insurance companies. If the Insurer is acting in a dishonest manner, delays processing the claim or fails to process a claim, refuses to settle a claim to minimize risk, or performs any other purposeful wrongdoing, then there is a potential bad faith claim available. Not only is the Insurer hurting the injured party but it is also hurting the Insured for not protecting the Insured as agreed upon in the contract that both parties signed.

We'll get into specific examples of types of bad faith claims and at the end of this chapter, but first it's important to setup the necessary elements that make a bad faith claim.

II. THE INSURER

A. ORIGIN

We can trace the concept of insuring vehicles back to China and as far back as 3,000 B.C. when agreements were found to cover goods on trade routes. Insurance is designed to cover risk of financial liability from loss of property or physical damages. The first insurance company in the United States was established in 1752 by Benjamin Franklin and was called the Philadelphia Contributionship.

Only horse and carriages were around during Benjamin Franklin's time. So, we need to fast forward to 1898 when Travelers issued the first insurance policy for a vehicle for Dr. Truman Martin. If there is ever a trivia question, it's important to note that Mr. Gilbert J. Loomis was technically the first person to buy an insurance policy, but there's debate as to whether the policy was applicable to a motor vehicle or a horse and buggy. (If you are interested, you can learn more at: http:dmv.org/articles/history-of-car-insurance.)

In 1925, Connecticut was the first state to pass a law which required motor vehicle owners to be able to prove that they could pay for damages and injuries caused to another in a motor vehicle accident. Since then, all states (including Missouri and Kansas) require motor vehicle insurance, except for New Hampshire, which does not require mandated insurance.

B. How the Insurer Makes Money

Insurance is all about managing risk. Insuring thousands of drivers moving at high speeds in metal boxes is a risky business. As a result, the Insurer does more than just take your monthly premiums to make money.

To maximize returns on taking substantial risks, the Insurer will conduct a risk-assessment on each individual driver which includes assessing: (a) the Insured's driving record, (v) where the Insured lives, and (c) the make, model, and year of the vehicle insured. From here, the Insurer pools policy holder's premiums together and pays expenses resulting from claims through the financial year and any other expenses. Then the Insurer will invest the pools of money into conservative instruments, like bonds and securities, and some into more of high-risk and high-reward investments.

The purpose of investing premium payments from the Insureds is two-fold. First, the investments make money and keep shareholders happy. Second, the investments keep premiums down for the Insureds. If the Insurer can keep premium payments at a reasonable rate, more consumers will take out policies with the Insurer; thus, increasing the Insurer's net income.

III. Types of Insurance and Coverages

Now that horse and carriages are a thing of the past (at least in the mainstream) and the majority of America elects to drive a motor vehicle, Kansas and Missouri have decided to make auto insurance and certain coverages mandatory. The specific coverages required by Kansas and Missouri are outlined below in subsection E.

A. Liability Insurance

Liability insurance is the basic type of insurance available. If You are involved in an accident, then this provides passengers in Your vehicle and, if You are at fault, the other driver to recover money from the motor vehicle collision. Basically, liability insurance covers damages that You caused.

There are two types of basic liability insurance. First, bodily injury liability covers an individual's physical injuries from a motor vehicle collision if You are at fault. Second, property damage covers Your legal responsibility for damages to property. Usually, this would be to the third-party's vehicle. But, it could also encompass trees, mailboxes, houses, city property, etc. For both types of liability insurance coverages, the Insurer will only pay-up to Your policy limits and nothing more.

B. Underinsured Motorist Insurance

Underinsured Motorist Coverage ("UIM") pays for medical expenses that result from a motor vehicle accident where the other driver has too little insurance to cover all the medical expenses.

For instance, Bob and Charlie are in a motor vehicle accident and both are insured. Bob suffered a broken leg and needs surgery to repair his tibia. Charlie's liability insurance is capped at $25,000. Bob's medical expenses, including post-surgery treatment, is in excess of the $25,000 limit of Charlie's policy. Bob will more than likely be able to collect the $25,000 from Charlie's insurance company, but what is Bob to do about his outstanding medical bills? Luckily for Bob, he has UIM coverage on his auto policy and is able to recoup his costs from his own policy up to his own policy's limits. UIM coverage also covers lost wages and pain and suffering.

C. Uninsured Motorist

Another important policy is Underinsured Motorist ("UM") coverage. This protects You from drivers who are driving without insurance.

Assume again that Bob and Charlie are in a motor vehicle accident. In this example, Bob doesn't have an active policy at the time of the collision. Charlie sustained physical injuries and lost wages because of the accident but cannot make a claim against Bob's Insurer because Bob doesn't have insurance. However, if Charlie elected UM coverage in his policy and he will be able to make a claim against his own insurance company to recoup his damages from his physical injuries and lost wages.

D. MEDICAL PAYMENTS/ PERSONAL INJURY PROTECTION

Medical Payments ("Med Pay") and Personal Injury Protection ("PIP") are in the same category of this chapter. They differ slightly but are similar enough to warrant cohabitation within the same subsection. Generally speaking, Med Pay covers all medical expenses and can function as medical coverage or supplement Your health insurance for medical costs. Med Pay, however, will not cover loss of income. PIP is similar to Med Pay but more comprehensive. Deductibles and co-pays apply to PIP, and some non-medical costs may be covered. State specific examples follow.

1. MISSOURI

Missouri is a Med Pay state. However, Missouri does not require Med Pay coverage. Unlike UIM/UM coverage, this coverage is not based on fault. Funds can be accessed for any injuries caused by any vehicle or accident. For example, if Charlie decided that it would be a smart decision to drive his 1989 Chevy Blazer through the woods at night and ended up hitting a tree resulting in a laceration on his forehead, he could make a Med Pay claim to recoup just his medical expenses related to the laceration (up to his Med Pay policy limits).

2. KANSAS

Kansas requires PIP coverage in an auto policy. Although PIP is similar to Missouri's Med Pay (i.e., coverage is not based on fault), PIP covers a wide variety of expenses that are not limited to medical expenses. The list includes disability/loss of income for a year, in-home services, funeral and burial or cremation expenses, and rehabilitation expenses.

E. Minimum Coverage

It is important for You to meet the minimum coverage requirements for Your state. Below are the minimum requirements for Missouri and Kansas. Please note, that while this chapter sets forth the minimum coverage requirements, it's recommended that You carefully consider Your coverage needs and exceed these minimum requirements if appropriate for Your situation.

1. Missouri

If You own or operate any motor vehicle in the state of Missouri, you must secure the following coverage (at a minimum):

1. $25,000 per person for bodily injury;
2. $50,000 per accident for bodily injury; and,
3. $10,000 per accident for property.

Additionally, Missouri requires UM coverage in the amount of $25,000 for bodily injury per person and $50,000 for bodily injury per accident.

2. Kansas

Similar to Missouri, Kansas requires that your liability insurance minimum is:

1. $25,000 for bodily injury per person;
2. $50,000 for bodily injury per vehicle; and,
3. $10,000 for property damage.

Kansas also requires PIP coverage which must meet minimums as well. As explained earlier, there are various categories PIP covers. The Kansas minimums for PIP coverage are:

1. $4,500 for medical expenses per person;
2. $900 for one year of disability and loss of income paid out once per month;
3. $25 for in-home services per day;
4. $2,000 for funeral, cremation or burial expenses; and,
5. $4,500 for rehabilitation.

In addition to the above, Kansas also requires UM and UIM coverage. Both of these coverages require the standard $25,000 for bodily injury per person and $50,000 for total injuries if several people in your car are hurt.

Additional coverages may be necessary above the state required minimum. For example, if You purchase or lease a new car, the lender may require You to have additional coverages or to have a higher minimum to reduce the lender's risk. Once again, minimizing risk for lenders and Insurers is how these companies stay in business.

F. Umbrella Excess

Umbrella Excess coverage is exactly what it sounds like. It provides an additional coverage or "excess liability" your policy limits. It protects not only bodily injury liability claims but also property damage claims. To understand this coverage, picture yourself at a local grocery store. When you enter, it's bright and sunny. However, when you leave it's pouring down rain. Without an umbrella, you're going to get drenched in rain water. It goes without saying, that the bigger the umbrella the more protected you are. This is how Umbrella Excess coverage works. It is designed to be there when the liability on all of your policies is exhausted. It goes above and beyond and covers situations that aren't generally covered such as certain lawsuits, personal liability situations, etc.

IV. Duties of the Insurer to the Insured

As discussed in Section I, one of the duties between the Insurer and Insured is a covenant of good faith and fair dealing. There are also statutory requirements (laws) that require the Insurer to perform certain acts or take certain measures on behalf of You, the Insured.

The first duty is the duty to indemnify. This requires the Insurer to pay for Your liability, up to the policy limits elected by You. This is a straightforward duty for the Insurer as this is the agreement that both parties made when the contract was signed.

The second duty, and much broader, is the promise to defend You. This requires the Insurer to hire legal counsel to defend You against any suit that is covered under the policy. This also covers all legal fees and costs. To determine whether there is a duty to defend, there must be a comparison of the "language of the insurance policy with the allegations in the complaint." *See, Trans World Airlines, Inc. v. Associated Aviation Underwriters*, 58 S.W.3d 609 (Mo. Ct. App. 2001). If the complaint, also called a lawsuit, gives rise to a claim that is within the types of liability covered by the insurance policy, then the insurer has a duty to defend. This right is controlled by rules and exceptions within the policy itself. Within these rules and exceptions sprout issues of whether a claim falls under Your policy.

V. How Bad Faith Litigation Comes into Play: First and Third Party Claims

This chapter has been focused on history, coverages, and duties of the Insurer. It's important to know everything that sets up a bad faith litigation claim before diving right into the heart of bad faith litigation. Picture this section as the climatic fight scene where our hero is taking on its villain.

The main crux of issues in bad faith litigation is the conduct of the Insurer with regard to You or a third-party (i.e. the person You injured). In order to prove a vexatious refusal claim or bad faith claim, the person bringing the claim has the burden to prove that the Insurer was acting in bad faith. *See, Mears v. Columbia Mut. Ins. Co.*, 855 S.W.2d 389 (Mo. Ct. App. 1993).

A. FIRST-PARTY CLAIMS: VEXATIOUS REFUSAL

A first-party claim is between an Insurer and the Insured. Generally, this occurs when the Insurer refuses to pay a claim that the Insured files with the Insurer's claims department and the claim is completely within the scope of the policy. It can also manifest in other ways; such as, refusing to accept a claim, ignoring a filed claim, or misleading the Insured. This is considered a vexatious refusal to pay; meaning, improper refusal for no just reason. A vexatious refusal to pay is brought under state law and must meet the elements required by state statute. (In Kansas suit will be brought under Kan. Stat. Ann. §40-2404, 256; In Missouri it will be brought under Mo. Rev. Stat. §375.420 with additional damages under § 375.296.)

An example of a vexatious refusal to pay is as follows: Kevin (the Insured) pays $2,500 out-of-pocket for medical expenses related to a motor vehicle collision. He then files a coverage claim to his Insurer to be reimbursed for his medical expenses. Kevin's Insurer only pays $1,000 claiming certain chiropractic treatment wasn't related to the accident nor necessary. However, the chiropractic treatment was directly related to the motor vehicle collision.

B. THIRD-PARTY CLAIMS: BAD FAITH CLAIMS

Third-party bad faith claims involve additional parties than are involved in a first-party claim. In third-party claims, we are dealing with the Insurer, Insured, and the injured party. Generally, this type of claim occurs when the Insurer refuses to settle a claim brought against its Insured which falls within policy scope. It can also manifest in other ways; such as, refusing to accept a claim, ignoring it, misleading the insured, etc., just as in a first-party claim.

n example of a bad faith claim is as follows: Daniel (the Injured Party) is injured in a motor vehicle accident that was caused by Vernon (the Insured) who is insured by the Insurer. Daniel hires

Super Attorney and his attorney submits a claim to Vernon's Insurer along with a demand of $50,000 for medical bills, lost wages, pain and suffering, and future medical costs. Vernon's liability insurance is capped at $50,000 and the claim is within the scope of the policy. However, the Insurer refuses to pay.

To bring a third-party claim, certain elements must be met and other common-law factors will influence the validity of the claim. (For a list of elements and factors see: Kansas-Bollinger v. Nuss, 449 P.2d 502 (Kan. 1969); Missouri Refusal to Settle-Shoby v. Kelly, 279 S.W. 3d 203 (Mo. Ct. App. 2009); Dyer v. General American Life Ins. Co., 541 S.W.3d 702 (Mo. Ct. App. 1976)).

There can also be a mixture of first-party claims and third-party claims. If Vernon's policy was only $25,000 and Daniel exhausted the policy limits of his claim, Daniel would need to turn to his own insurance company to recover more by using his UIM coverage.

C. What to do When Issues Arise

Damages can be severe in bad faith litigation to the Insurer if the Insurer was in fact acting in bad faith. Each case is unique because a court and a jury may award extra damages to a plaintiff beyond the policy limits to act as a punishment for an Insurer acting with knowingly ill will. For example, recently a California jury found that an Insurer's offer of $10,000 for the wrongful death of a child, when the policy limits were $300,000, was in bad faith and the jury awarded $3.9 million in punitive damages to the parents. See, *Clayton v. United Services Automobile Assn.*, 54 Call. App. 4th, 1158, 63 Cal. Rptr. 2d 419 (1997).

If issues arise when dealing with the Insurer it is best to seek the professional services of an attorney to help navigate the complexities, state law, and common-law in order to receive the just compensation that You deserve. A bad faith claim arises from a tort; which means that someone was wronged by another person. Whether it's Your Insurer delaying Your medical payments coverage or an Insurer undervaluing a wrongful death claim, it's imperative to seek professional legal assistance to make sure Your interests are protected.

ABOUT THE AUTHOR

José M. Bautista
Partner, Bautista LeRoy LLC
www.bautistaleroy.com
(816) 221-0382

José M. Bautista is a partner and founding member of Bautista LeRoy. José's practice consists of plaintiff's personal injury law, with an emphasis on railroad crossing litigation and police brutality cases. He has been recognized by the Kansas City Business Journal as "Best of the Bar," distinguished by Martindale-Hubbell as "AV Preeminent" for the highest level of professional excellence, and recently awarded the Vanguard Award by Asian American Bar Association of Kansas City (AABAKC). He is a former Chair of the Railroad Litigation Section of the national plaintiff's bar organization, the American Association for Justice, and former President of the AABAKC. José currently serves as a Fellow of the Bar for the Kansas City Metropolitan Bar Association and board member of the Legal Aid of Western Missouri.

CHAPTER 9:
Auto Accident Attorneys

By: Anthony S. McDaniel

I. INTRODUCTION: CHECKLIST FOR AFTER A CAR ACCIDENT

Unfortunately, car accidents are a fact of life. Many people do not realize just how dangerous it can be to operate a vehicle. However, with over 5 million non-fatal accidents a year in the U.S. and over 33,000 deaths annually, car accidents are a leading cause of death and injury across the country. So, statistically speaking, most drivers will be involved in some type of car accident during their lives. Taking the proper precautions when driving can help reduce the chance of an auto accident. Even with these precautions, there are some instances where an accident is unavoidable, even for the most attentive drivers.

Knowing what steps to take after a motor vehicle collision can help you stay focused and improve your chances of obtaining compensation for any injuries. After an accident most people have trouble remaining calm. Being involved in a collision with another vehicle can cause you to go into a state of shock. Keeping your cool during this situation has several benefits. While waiting for help to arrive, you can go over a mental checklist regarding the accident or better yet, write this checklist in your "notes" on your smartphone. Below are some important things that should be on this checklist.

A. Getting to Safety is Vital

The first thing you must do after an auto accident is get to safety. If the car is still drivable you need to move it so other motorists can get around the scene of the accident. In some instances, the car will be a hazard because of leaking fluids. When this happens, walk as far away as you can. Distance between yourself and the damaged car is important and something that you should take seriously. Make sure you can still see your vehicle and remain on the "scene." By walking to a safe spot you will be able to get your bearings and figure out your next move.

B. Call the Authorities

Once you are in a safe spot, you need to call the local authorities. Sometimes they can give you an idea regarding how long it will be before they arrive. Once the authorities arrive, they will make a report of what happened. A detailed police report is worth its weight in gold if you are the victim of the accident and seek compensation. This report will include, among other things, a sketch of the accident and testimony from witnesses who saw what happened prior to the car accident.

In some cases, where injuries are not apparent or serious, the authorities will not write a report on scene. If this happens, first request that the officer write a report. If you are told that it is not possible at the time, ask the officer how you can file a report with the police station. Then you need to go to the police station, fill out a police report, and give your statement. This step is very important if you believe you were not at fault for the accident. You need to get the facts written down because drivers' stories can change as time passes.

C. Avoid Discussing Fault With the Other Party

A big mistake that some drivers make after a car accident is discussing fault with the other party. No one likes admitting when they are wrong. This type of confrontation will usually not end well. Instead of arguing at the scene of the accident, you should remain silent until the authorities arrive. Then give your statement away from the other driver.

D.   Contact Your Insurance Company

Contacting your insurance company allows you to arrange a tow for the car if needed and discuss the details of what happened. For most people, getting their damaged car back on the road in a hurry is essential. The faster you get the ball rolling on a tow and the subsequent repairs, the easier you will find it to get back behind the wheel.

II.   Your Smartphone Is an Important Tool

As the familiar saying goes: A picture is worth a thousand words. When it comes to car accidents, this is definitely true.

These days, most people don't leave home without a smartphone. In the event of a motor vehicle collision, your smartphone's camera is an incredibly important tool for gathering crucial evidence in your personal injury case. Before smartphones were in nearly every person's purse or pocket, evidence gathering was reserved for police officers and insurance adjusters. Police officers prepared their reports and snapped a few photos. In some cases, an accident investigator would visit the accident site to collect evidence several hours or days after it happened. Now, drivers can take photos documenting the scene and gather eyewitness statements almost immediately after an accident.

Obviously, the first step for a car accident victim is to get medical attention for any injuries. However, if you are physically well enough to gather evidence there are several ways a smartphone can help a future personal injury case.

A.   Record Your Observations

Smartphones and many cell phones allow you to record voices, memos, and videos. Use this function or app to record your personal observations of the accident scene. Use descriptive language and include as much detail as possible. Document your observations of the weather, your injuries, vehicle damage, and how the accident occurred.

B. Take Plenty of Photos

Photographs play a crucial role in personal injury cases. Take as many photos as you can, including images of the scene, the vehicles involved in the accident, tire marks in the road, broken glass, traffic lights, road signs, and any injuries you sustained.

Take photos completely around each vehicle. Start on the driver's side and walk around the vehicle, taking a photo every two steps. This will give you, the police, the insurance company, and your attorney the best chance to see the damage.

When it comes to injuries, remember that bruises and other injuries tend to worsen as time passes. Continue taking photos of bruises and other personal injuries in the days following your accident. You do not need to take ten photos of the injuries on the same day. Rather, taking one or two photos for ten days is a better way to document the injury.

C. Gather Statements from Eyewitness

If any pedestrians or other motorists observed the crash, ask for their information and, if possible, write down a personal statement of their observations. It's important to capture an observer's statement as soon as possible following an accident because a person's memory may change over time.

III. The Importance of the Police Report

One of the most powerful tools you after an accident is a police report which is written and recorded at the scene of an accident. There are several things included in a police report which are extremely helpful when collecting damages due to an accident.

A. Statements from the Parties Involved

Statements from all the parties involved in an accident are extremely helpful when deciding who is at fault. The report hopefully contains statements from the drivers in the accident and any witness who were nearby at the time of impact. Reading these statements allows an insurance adjuster, judge, or jury to paint a picture of what happened and who is to blame for the damage.

B. Diagrams of the Scene of the Accident

Sometimes the first officer to arrive will make a rough sketch of what he/she sees. If it is a very serious collision, the officer may take pictures or call in a team that specializes in accident reconstruction. Having a detailed analysis of the scene of the accident is invaluable to the injured party who seeks compensation.

C. Conclusions Regarding Fault

In most cases, the officer who is working the accident will include a brief narrative in his/her report about his/her opinions on fault. A police officer's opinion regarding who and what caused the accident adds legitimacy to the claims made by the injured party. The officer will also detail whether any citations were given and note who was cited.

D. The Injuries and Damages

A police report will also include a breakdown of the injuries and damages from the accident. Both the type of injury and the severity are recorded. A special section is reserved on the report that indicates whether an ambulance was needed and notes which individual(s) was/were transported from the scene in the emergency vehicle. Because of the amount of information in this report, the victim of the accident needs the report to get what he/she is entitled to for his/her injuries.

IV. Waiting Too Long Can Cost You

If are injured in a car accident due to another person's negligence, you probably have a lot of questions. Do you have a case? Are your injuries severe enough to deserve compensation? How much is this going to cost you? Do you really want to get involved in a lawsuit?

These are all normal questions. An injury can leave anyone feeling overwhelmed and anxious. Unfortunately, far too many people wait until it is too late to present their questions to a personal injury attorney. Frequently, car accident injury victims delay speaking to an attorney because they don't want to seem like they're complaining or out to "make a quick buck." So, they hesitate to call an attorney. They don't want to be perceived as "one of those people" who files a lawsuit after a motor vehicle collision.

As time passes, however, they continue to suffer physical pain as medical bills pile up. In some cases, they finally contact an attorney, only to discover that too much time has passed to bring a claim. In other cases, the long delay has hurt their chances of receiving full and fair compensation for their injuries.

A. Statute of Limitations

If you have been injured, it's critical to talk to a personal injury attorney as soon as possible after your accident. Waiting too long can actually prevent you from ever filing a claim. The law places strict deadlines on how long you have to file a personal injury case. This deadline, known as a "statute of limitations," prevents people from suing years after an accident occurred. The law does not allow you to wait decades before bringing a lawsuit. So, speak to an attorney right away to determine how long you have to file a case.

B. Loss of Evidence

Lengthy delays can hurt your case even if you file within the statute of limitations. To prove your case, you need to show evidence that you were injured, that your injury was caused by the defendant's negligence, and that you suffered damages as a result of the defendant's negligence. It's best to collect evidence, including witness statements, medical reports, and physical evidence (photos, etc.), as close as possible to the time of the accident. If you wait too long, there is a good chance the evidence will degrade over time.

C. Undiscovered Injuries

Don't automatically assume that you are not injured. Many people experience a surge of adrenaline during a car accident which can mask injury symptoms. Also, some car accident injuries can take several days or even weeks to manifest symptoms.

D. Forced Quick Settlements

Be wary of speaking to an insurance company without first consulting an attorney. Insurers may send an adjuster to the scene of an accident. They may hire an investigator to conduct surveillance on you and family. They may record the telephone call without your consent. This is sometimes done in an attempt to offer you a settlement worth far less than you deserve. Remember that the insurance company makes money primarily on reducing the amounts paid on claims. Experienced personal injury attorneys are familiar with these strategies and can help you safeguard your legal rights against insurance company pressure tactics.

V. Valuing Your Claim

One of the most common questions car accident injury plaintiffs ask is: how much my case is worth? The answer isn't as straightforward as you might think. However, an experienced personal injury attorney can usually give you a good idea of the general value of your case.

Several factors determine how much compensation you can expect to receive. Both your attorney and the defense – usually an insurance company – will try to figure out the amount of compensation you may receive at a trial.

This doesn't mean that your case will go to trial. Rather, it helps the two sides determine an appropriate figure for settlement purposes. In fact, the majority of personal injury cases settle. Despite this fact, it's still important to work with an attorney who is willing to take your case all the way to trial if necessary.

To arrive at a reasonable value for your injuries, your attorney will consider many things, including:

- The type of accident (semi-truck accident, multiple vehicle accident, etc.);
- The nature and severity of your injuries;
- How your injury affects your income and career;
- Whether your injuries are short-term or long-term;
- Your out-of-pocket expenses;
- Do you bear some fault for the accident;
- Your long-term prognosis.

Because no two cases are exactly alike, your attorney may consider other factors unique to your case.

It's natural, after an accident, to worry about mounting medical bills, lost wages, and a potentially permanent change in your lifestyle. However, it's best to take time to consult with an experienced attorney rather than accept a quick settlement offered by an insurance company. Your attorney has your best interests in mind, whereas the insurance company is concerned only with protecting its bottom line.

Although most cases settle, there are times when it's necessary to have a trial. In these cases, the jury will ultimately decide how much compensation you receive. Some people mistakenly believe that the judge makes this decision, but this is incorrect. After the jury hears both sides of the case and reviews all the evidence, your attorney and the defense will each have an opportunity to talk to the jury about damages. This is your attorney's chance to convince the jury that the evidence shows you are entitled to a certain amount of compensation.

This is also why it's critically important to choose the right attorney for your case.

VI. Ways Your Attorney Can Help

Being involved in a car accident can be difficult. Between property damage and personal injuries, you can quickly become overwhelmed. One of the main concerns you may have is when will you be able to get the situation settled and move on with their life.

A. Providing an Estimated Timeline

Your attorney can evaluate the situation and determine if compensation is possible. Most people have unrealistic expectations when it comes to the time it will take to get their case settled. There are several factors that come into play when trying to obtain a settlement following a car accident. In many cases, the other party will contest who was at fault or the nature and extent of any injuries. When this happens, there will be a variety of things that will need to happen before a settlement can be reached. Your attorney understands all these factors will help you get a realistic understanding of how long your car accident case is going to take.

B. Giving You Time to Complete All Necessary Medical Treatments

You should complete all necessary medical treatments that relate to the injuries sustained in the accident. Once you completed these treatments, your attorney will obtain a copy of your medical records and bills. Your attorney will also help you determine the value of the lost wages you suffered as a result of the injuries from the accident. This information is critical to the value your claim. Settling before this information available and understood may result in receiving less than fair compensation.

C. Helping You to Avoid Lengthy Settlement Negotiations

Once your attorney has all the key documents and evidence, he/she will send a demand letter to the insurance company. This letter details the case and the compensation that is sought. Your attorney will put the insurance company "on the clock" and demand an answer within a certain period of days. During this time, your attorney will work closely with the insurance adjuster on the case to get them to accept the top figure you seek.

D. Filing a Lawsuit

If settlement negotiations are not successful, your attorney will file a lawsuit on your behalf. The court will set a trial date for a year or so after the lawsuit is filed. During this year, the insurance company (or defense attorneys) and your attorney will work feverishly to reach a settlement that helps both sides. If a settlement cannot be reached during this year, then the case will go to trial. A jury will decide how much

compensation, if any, you get for your injuries. Oftentimes, the best case outcome for all parties is to settle a case before the court date. Your attorney will work to get this matter resolved and to get you the money you need to get on with your life.

VII. Elements of a Personal Injury Case

A. Negligence

Negligence is something you hear a lot about on television and in the media, but do you really know what it means? If you've been injured in a car accident caused by another person, you will probably hear it. Despite being a relatively straightforward term, negligence can be a complicated legal concept because each state has a different standard of negligence.

In Missouri, the legal definition of negligence is a breach of the duty of care that causes injury. To prove negligence, a plaintiff (the injured person who filed the lawsuit) must prove four things:

1. The existence of a duty of care;
2. A breach of the duty of care;
3. An injury;
4. Causation between the breach and the injury;

To fully comprehend the definition of negligence, it helps to understand the role of each element within the context of a personal injury case.

1. THE DUTY OF CARE

From an early age, most of us are taught to treat others as we ourselves would like to be treated. This "Golden Rule" is more than just good manners – it ensures that everyone gets an opportunity to live and work in a safe society without constant fear of injury.

The legal "duty of care" is a similar concept. The courts determine the applicable "duty of care". In Missouri, the laws require a driver to use a degree of care that a "very careful person" would use. On the other hand, passengers and pedestrians are held to a "reasonable person" standard. That is, they ask themselves what a reasonable person would have done given similar circumstances.

Because every case involves different facts, the standards change depending on the people and situations involved. There are different standards of care for professionals too. For example, architects are held to the same standard of care as other licensed architects in their communities. Similarly, heart surgeons have a duty to deliver the same standard of care as other heart surgeons in their geographic area. Minors in Missouri are held to the same standard of care as other children of like age, intelligence and maturity. Understanding the different standards of care will help you and your attorney evaluate the worth of your case.

2. THE BREACH OF THE DUTY OF CARE

When someone's conduct falls below the required standard of care, a breach occurs. However, not all breaches of the duty of care are automatic cases of negligence. The breach must cause an injury, which refers to the "causation" element of negligence.

3. CAUSAL CONNECTION

Causation is a critical element in a negligence case and refers to the connection between the breach of the duty of care and the resulting injury to the plaintiff. The defendant (the party who breached the duty of care) can act negligently all day long, but if his or her actions don't result in an injury to the plaintiff, the plaintiff does not have a case for negligence against the defendant.

VIII. HOW YOUR ATTORNEY WILL WORK TO PROVE NEGLIGENCE

The injuries that can result from an auto accident can be quite extensive. If you are the victim of a car accident, then you will have to work hard to get the compensation you need. In order for your attorney to get you the results you are after, he/she has to prove that the other party in the accident acted in a negligent manner. While this may seem simple, it is anything but. The following are some of methods that your attorney will use when trying to prove negligence in a car accident personal injury case.

A. TRAFFIC LAWS ARE DUTIES OF CARE

Simply put, a driver's duty of care is an obligation he/she has to other motorists on the roadways. For instance, if a person ran a red light and then caused an accident, that person would be considered negligent if a jury determined that he violated his duty of care. Everyday traffic laws are duties of care and ignoring them is one of the most common examples of violating of your duty of care to other drivers. It should be noted that the severity of the injuries sustained in an accident is not considered when trying to establish whether a defendant had a duty of care towards the plaintiff in the case.

B. Pre-existing Conditions

If you are injured in a car accident, then you must prove that the driver of the other car caused your injuries. This can be a lot easier said than done you've been in multiple accidents in your life or have pre-existing conditions. Your attorney must explain to the jury which injuries are related to the accident (or exacerbated by) and which are not.

Working with a personal injury attorney will help you get more information regarding what you need to prove and how difficult it will be to separate prior injuries from your current injuries. If suing for damages done to the vehicle, the same principles will apply. A jury must be able to see that the injuries and damages you have were unequivocally caused by the defendant before a judgement is awarded.

IX. How Your Attorney Gets Paid

Whether you are commuting to work, taking children to school, or simply running errands, you spend a significant portion of each week behind the wheel. Although car accidents happen frequently, they can wreak havoc on multiple aspects of your life. Many car accident victims worry how they will afford to work with an attorney. They may even hesitate to contact an attorney because they assume they won't be able to pay the fee.

Fortunately, many personal injury attorneys charge nothing up front. Instead, they work on a contingency fee basis, which allows you to pay nothing out of pocket. The attorney only receives compensation if the attorney recovers money on your behalf, at which time you pay the attorney a percentage of the personal injury settlement.

X. Conclusion

If you have been involved in a car accident, you are likely dealing with bodily injuries, pain and suffering, and expenses from time off work and medical bills. Additionally, you may be confronting various mental concerns, such as post-traumatic stress and emotional distress. Understandably, you may have numerous questions. That is why, if you are injured in a car accident, it's critical that you to talk to a personal injury attorney as soon as possible after your accident.

ABOUT THE AUTHOR

Anthony S. McDaniel
Attorney, Bautista LeRoy LLC
www.bautistaleroy.com
Tel: (816) 221-0382

Anthony S. McDaniel is an associate at Bautista LeRoy. He focuses his practice on plaintiff's personal injury law and concentrates on motor vehicle accidents. Anthony refreshed the basic motor vehicle collision approach with innovative investigation, negotiation, and demand drafting techniques in a political climate increasingly embracing tort reform. By navigating insurance company policies and developing creative arguments to get the most out of each policy, Anthony established a successful practice harnessed in efficiency and precision. He was awarded the Harry S. Truman Leadership Award in 2015 and recognized among his graduating class as one of the most decorated trial team members. He is a member of the Order of the Barristers, and is involved in the Association for Women Lawyers, Kansas City Metropolitan Bar Association and the Jackson County Bar Association.

CHAPTER 10:
Nursing Home Neglect Attorneys

By: Andrew LeRoy

I. Introduction: Nursing Home Neglect Overview

Making a nursing home choice for your loved is very emotional. It is time consuming, exhausting, and research intensive. In Missouri, there is great difficulty finding the correct nursing home. Research shows that Missouri is one of the worst states in the nation for nursing home care. Families for Better Health Care gave Missouri a failing grade and ranked the Show Me State fourth-to-last in their rankings. See, http://www.cbsnews.com/news/eleven-states-get-failing-grades-for-nursing-home-care/; http://nursinghomereportcards.com/state/mo/. Deciding whether a nursing home is the correct choice for a loved one or which one to choose is emotionally taxing but to know that Missouri has been ranked in the bottom of the entire nation makes the decision even harder. However, not all nursing home in Missouri are in rough shape and some even go above-and-beyond what is expected out of a nursing home.

Improper care in nursing homes can lead to devastating consequences and can easily be avoided by families putting time into their selection of a nursing home and visiting their family member often. This chapter will discuss what to look for in a nursing home, what to do if injury occurs, how to find an attorney to handle a nursing home abuse case, and the most popular nursing home cases that are adjudicated in courts.

II. Types of Nursing Home Cases

Nursing home claims comes from many different sources that cause physical and emotional injuries. The types of neglect range widely because of the personal and intimate relationship a nursing home has with its residents.

1. Pressure Sores

Most commonly referred to as "bed sores", pressure sores are caused when there is pressure to the skin—usually a part of the body where the bone is close to the surface of the skin—that goes unrelieved for an extended amount of time. This causes the skin where the bone and skin are meeting to have pressure build. The sore will then become an open wound, become infected, and slowly turn "crater-like" in appearance similar to a blister. Ultimately, the infection will spread into healthy parts of the skin and then the wound will continue to spread; exposing muscles, tendons, and bones.

This is common in nursing homes and hospitals because of the sedentary lifestyle caused by both places. To prevent pressure sores, it's important that the individual repositions every 15 minutes. Common areas where pressure sores occur are:

1. Buttocks
2. Spine and shoulder blades
3. Back of arms and legs where in contact with a wheelchair or bed
4. The head area including the ears
5. Lower back and hips
6. Knees, heels, and ankles

It's important to watch to make sure that there are no red spots showing up on your loved one and to make sure that the nursing home staff is properly moving and turning over your loved one.

2. FALLS

Nursing home falls that result in wrongful deaths have increased at an alarming rate. In 2005, the rate of wrongful death from unintentional falls was just below 44%. This rate rose significantly by 2014 increasing to 58%. If this statistic isn't speaking volumes to you right now, remember that these are only the *reported* falls from nursing homes. Some nursing homes don't report any falls or minor falls so this number may be higher.

Each nursing home should have a fall assessment on each of their clients which includes physical health, previous falls, and medications taken so that caregivers understand how the individual will react to daily activities and walking. All residents should have proper foot wear with grips on the bottom of their slippers, shoes, socks in addition to the necessary walking aids (i.e. cane, walker, etc.).

A high-danger zone where residents fall is climbing in and out of their beds. It's important to know whether the bed is at the correct height for the resident and if the rails are properly fastened to the bed. It's easy for a resident to fall while trying to get out or into bed. Caregivers should also help residents up when necessary and call for additional help when getting a resident to turn over in bed to prevent bed sores, to get out of bed, or for walking.

When falls do occur, it can be devastating for the resident and their quality of life. A fall can cause broken bones, head injuries—which can be exasperated because of any medication the resident is on—and stress and anxiety wondering whether they will fall again. It's imperative that if a resident falls, he or she is seen by a doctor immediately to see if there is any head trauma, internal bleeding, or broken bones.

3. Caregiver Neglect

Caregiver neglect encompasses many scenarios that are extremely important to the everyday quality of life of a resident. This type of neglect includes personal hygiene such as brushing teeth, having clean clothes and underwear, and bathing. There are also basic needs such as food, water, and a living area that is regularly cleaned. Additionally, there are medical needs such as: (1) giving adequate medication, (2) remember to give medication, or (3) providing necessary medication for the resident. This type of neglect is the most common in nursing homes.

Medication errors happen when there are mistakes while preparing the medication and/or giving the medication to the residents. There are many ways an error can occur but some of the more common ways include:

1. A nurse can give too much or not enough medication to a resident
2. Incorrect medicine or failure to give require medicine
3. Expired medicine
4. Failure to provide medication at required time intervals per doctor's orders

Caregiver neglect also encompasses improper supervision of residents. Improper supervision depends on the needs of the resident. If a resident has mental issues that cause him or her to forget where he or she is and are prone to wander off or if he or she has a history of falling but caregivers allow the resident to walk on his or her own and the resident falls, that's improper supervision.

Because caregiver neglect covers many different scenarios it becomes difficult to distinguish if there is neglect, the type of neglect, and how long it has been going on. Depending on the situation you may notice behavioral changes, dehydration, weight loss, hygiene issues, etc. You can also spot other types of neglect by noticing other residents in the nursing home and the nursing home itself.

4. SEXUAL ABUSE

Unfortunately, sexual abuse in nursing homes is all too common. Sexual abuse is defined in Missouri as, "subject[ing] another person to sexual contact when that person is incapacitated, incapable of consent, or lacks capacity of consent, or by use of forcible compulsion." *See*, RSMo §566.100(1). The types of sexual abuse can range from inappropriate touching to rape and often goes unnoticed by family members and underreported.

There are a variety of reasons for sexual abuse to go unreported. First, the most typical victim in nursing home sexual abuse are residents who have medical conditions that make their speech or non-verbal cues difficult to express. Any form of memory loss such as dementia will also exasperate the issue. Family members might not be actively involved in their day-to-day lives and visits may be infrequent so they have no one to talk to and lack the resources to empower themselves. Victims may also feel threatened by their attacker because they are the one giving them the care that they so desperately need.

Signs that sexual abuse is occurring are:

1. Unexplained blood stains
2. Bleeding, infection, and/or bruising around the genitalia
3. Bruising, hand prints, or scratches anywhere on the body
4. Increased anxiety and fear when particular staff members or fellow-residents are nearby

Even if the victim has excellent communication skills and are void of any medical issues that would frustrate reporting the abuse, a victim may feel embarrassed or that he or she has no power because of his or her situation and will not report the abuse. Even when the abuse is reported to the nursing home staff, most complaints often fail to be followed-up by the management; thus, goes uninvestigated.

5. Malnutrition

Malnutrition and dehydration is a common nursing home neglect issue. This happens when the nursing home doesn't give a resident a well-balanced meal. If a resident is receiving the same meal for breakfast, lunch, and dinner, he or she is missing out on critically important vitamins and minerals that are necessary for the brain and body to function.

It is common sense that an individual should receive a well-balanced meal for breakfast, lunch, and dinner. If you were to miss out on breakfast and didn't eat until lunch, you would feel light headed, possibly have a headache, and be tired until you ate something for lunch. Likewise, if you ate the same meal three times a day you would miss out on many other important nutrients.

Surprisingly, one-third of all nursing home residents suffer from malnutrition or dehydration. This can lead to severe medical issues. A resident's medication may require him or her to have a full meal and water before ingesting or his or her body becomes weak and the bones become brittle. This increases the risk of a fall and more severe injuries.

Malnutrition generally stems from improper staffing and inadequate individual attention to the resident. Each caregiver, on average, is required to help between 7-15 residents eat and drink during meal time depending on the meal. Another reason for malnutrition is lack of choices for meals and snacks and poor dental hygiene.

It's important to watch your loved one for signs of malnutrition. Obvious signs are weight loss, muscular problems with fatigue, poor muscle strength, and skin changes.

6. Emotional and Psychological Abuse

Physical abuse is often easier to detect than emotional and psychological abuse. But, emotional and psychological abuse may be the most common type of abuse in nursing home neglect. It's hard to detect because it gradually causes damage to the victim and sometimes the victim doesn't even recognize that the abuse is present.

The types of abuse that can come from emotional and psychological abuse are:

1. Ignoring the victim
2. Humiliating, ridiculing and/or minimizing the victim
3. Isolating the victim from events, friends, or family
4. Blaming the victim for events that are not his or her fault or doing
5. Intimidation of the victim
6. Manipulation of the victim

Because you are not with your loved one all the time, it is hard to see whether there has been emotional or psychological abuse. Some factors to look for are:

1. Eye contact avoidance
2. Low self-esteem
3. Disturbed, scared, anxious, depressed, withdrawn, or any similar behavior
4. Mood swings
5. Changes in sleep pattern
6. New twitches (i.e. nail biting, rocking, mumbling, etc.)

Unfortunately, this type of abuse takes a while to develop. Sometimes emotional and psychological abuse can have an immediate impact on the individual's daily life and other times it may take months for signs of abuse to show. It's important to have constant contact with your loved one to establish a pattern as to how he or she reacts toward certain caregivers, what a "bad day" looks for your loved one, and to establish a baseline so if there are any deviations in behavior you will notice. In this type of abuse, it is better for you to be proactive rather than reactionary.

III. What Can You Do?

If you suspect your loved one has experienced some type of nursing home abuse, it's important that you take the correct steps to report any abuse immediately. Below are some steps that you and your family can take to put your loved one in the right situation.

1. Deciding on a Nursing Home

Once the decision is made to place your loved one in the care of a nursing home, you and your family need to research which nursing home is the right choice. This decision goes beyond the aesthetics of a nursing home and into the very heart of a nursing home's core operation. It's important to take your time researching the correct nursing home and the types of services your loved one needs.

2. How Much Care Is Needed?

There are different types of nursing homes that offer a different amount of care. The traditional notion is that all nursing homes are 24-hour intensive care which may detract potential-residents from entertaining the idea of a nursing home. However, each nursing home is different. Some are independent living homes where residents can move about freely. Some are 24-hour intensive care which assist with each resident every hour of the day. Some are a hybrid of these two. In Missouri, there are residential care facilities (RCF), assisted living facilities (ALF), intermediate care facilities (ICF), skilled nursing facilities, and long-term care units which operate within hospitals. See, http://health.mo.gov/seniors/nursinghomes/licensecert.php. RCF is more independent than ALF and ICF but as you go further down the list, your loved one will receive more intensive care in the nursing home.

It is important to identify how much care is needed for your loved one, how much care will be needed in the future, and what types of services you should look for in a nursing home. Understanding what type of care your loved one truly needs is important. If your loved one needs 24-hour care, then it would be unwise to select an independent nursing home where injury is more probable.

There are also additional services beyond the standard room, meals, nurse supervision, medical care, and social activities. If your loved one requires special therapy or transportation to a physical therapist or doctor regularly, then you should look for a nursing home with additional services to help assist your loved one.

3. MAKING A CHOICE

When a decision is made to put your loved one in a home, ask for recommendations from family members and friends. Ask if they like a particular nursing home or—sometimes, more importantly—which nursing homes to avoid. If you cannot find any recommendations, the next best step is to do a search online. Missouri offers a search engine for any city or zip code in the state as does Medicare. See, http://health.mo.gov/safety/showmelongtermcare/ or https://www.medicare.gov/nursinghomecompare/search.html.

Once you narrow down the list of nursing homes it's important to verify they have accreditation or certification. You may request the nursing home to show proof of certification and verify it with Missouri's Senior & Disability Services. Go ahead and check out the ratings on a particular nursing home online and ask around to see if you can find someone who has experience with a particular nursing home.

Much like selecting a college, it's important to take a "campus tour" before committing to a nursing home. Schedule an official tour with the staff but also drop by unannounced to evaluate the staff and nursing home when they aren't expecting to give a tour. Engage with residents to see if they are happy and if the facility is maintained. What is the staff to resident ratio? Are staff members friendly or are they unengaged with residents? Ask difficult questions to the staff and especially the management. Because staff members are the primary reason nursing home abuse happens, ask the manager if they do background checks on their staff and inquire about the hiring process.

A website click and view will never supplant physically being in the nursing home and looking with your own two-eyes. It's important you take your time to decide what type of care your loved one needs and which nursing home will truly be the best. The time it takes to find a nursing home may be taxing on you or your family, but patience is the key to make sure your loved one is truly going to be loved in their next home.

3. IF INJURY OCCURS

If abuse occurs or you suspect abuse, you should document each episode immediately and ask your loved one about the circumstances. It's important to get all the information written down and take pictures or video, if applicable. Once you talk to your love one about the situation and secured any evidence here are steps you need to take.

> (a) Report the abuse or potential abuse immediately. Missouri has an Adult Abuse and Neglect Hotline at 1-800-392-0210. Anyone can report abuse if he or she believes that someone is being abused; however, some professionals are mandated by law to report. After a report is filed, Adult Protective Services (APS) or law enforcement may respond to your report depending on your loved one's needs and situation.
>
> (b) Secure all the rights given to you.
>
> (c) Find an attorney and file a civil lawsuit if necessary.

4. FILE A CIVIL LAWSUIT: FINDING AN ATTORNEY

When you look for an attorney to provide justice for the hurt and grief your family suffered due to nursing home neglect there are a couple things to keep mind when researching attorneys.

The attorney needs to have a background in and experience with nursing home neglect cases. If an attorney does not advertise on his or her website that he or she handles nursing home abuse matters, then you should continue your search. Nursing home abuse cases are tricky to navigate and inexperienced attorneys may have difficulty picking up on the nuances associated with these claims.

Always meet with the attorney or attorneys before signing a contract. You need to get a feel for the attorneys both as professionals and as individuals. Nursing home abuse cases deal with personal matters and our loved ones. If an attorney seems distant or uninterested this is a sign that he or she may not give your loved one the attention he or she deserves.

5. Criminal Prosecution

The National Institute of Justice found that the older the victim, the less likely the offender would be convicted. Additionally, if there is no physical trauma evidence (i.e. bruises, cuts, etc.) the less likely a victim is believed. Therefore, it's imperative that you document the abuse the moment you begin to suspect. Take a journal with you each time you go to visit your loved one and takes notes about the facility, your loved one's attitude and mannerisms, and anything else that you notice.

IV. Conclusion

From the beginning of the nursing home selection process all the way through your loved one being in a nursing home, the key is patience and time. The best way to prevent nursing home abuse of any kind is to do research in advance and take time to make a careful choice. Once your choice is made, check in on your loved one to make sure that he or she receives the adequate care and are treated well.

ABOUT THE AUTHOR

Andrew S. LeRoy
Partner, Bautista LeRoy LLC
www.bautistaleroy.com
(816) 221-0382

Andrew S. LeRoy is a partner and founding member of Bautista LeRoy. Andrew focuses his practice on plaintiff's personal injury law. Andrew's practice concentrates on motor vehicle accidents, hunting accidents, sex abuse and nursing home negligence cases. Andrew enjoys fighting insurance companies, zealously advocating for his clients to get the most out of each insurance policy. He was recognized as KCMBA Young Lawyer of the Year in 2014. He is the current President of the KCMBA's Solo Practitioner/Small Firm Section.

CHAPTER 11:
Consumer Attorneys

By: Michael Rapp

I. Introduction

Consumer law is special. It differs from many other areas of the law because it has attorney fees built into it. If you sue a company for cheating you and a court determines the company did something wrong, not only do they owe you money and have to fix the problem they caused, but they may have to pay for your lawyer on top of it.

To advise a person on finding a consumer lawyer, the most important thing is to know when you need one. When you look in the yellow pages or on the Internet, lawyers are grouped into categories (such as, personal injury, estate planning, criminal defense, or bankruptcy). Only recently have you seen a category entitled "consumer law." Most people can easily recognize when they are injured, or when they get pulled over, or accused of a crime. In these situations, they know they need some help. While these are all specialized areas of law, there are in most areas, many attorneys to choose from and the challenge is finding the best one for you. Consumer law is something created in the past 50 years and often isn't taught in law school. Finding a consumer lawyer is a bit more complicated. First, you need to know if you need one. Second, you need to find the right one. This Chapter will help you determine when you should look for a consumer lawyer.

II. What is a Consumer Lawyer?

There is a common saying among attorneys: you don't choose the area of law you practice, it choses you. In most states, there is not a formal certification process for different types of lawyers. This means that attorneys self-identify what type of law practice they practice based upon their experience. In other words, what they do most often, is what kind of lawyer they are.

That is not to say that the process is completely informal. Most lawyers belong to organizations that support the area of the law they practice. Those organizations often hold conferences with continuing education classes. This allows lawyers from around the country to share experience and learn from one another to become more advanced and proficient in their chosen area of the law. These organizations not only serve as repositories of best practices and scholarship, but also help lawyers inform the legislature and regulatory bodies on the current state of the law.

For consumer lawyers, there is one major organization: The National Association of Consumer Advocates ("NACA"). NACA is a nonprofit, nationwide organization of more than 1,500 attorneys who have represented hundreds of thousands of consumers victimized by fraudulent, abusive, and predatory business practices. NACA lawyers take an oath when they join that they will not take cases for any business or commercial client that would put them opposite consumers. This means that they promise never to take on a case where they would sue a person on behalf of a company. As you can imagine, big business pays well so that is quite a big promise. Not all lawyers that are familiar with consumer law belong to NACA; but the authors of this chapter, and every lawyer in their firm, do. Several times a year, the lawyers at our firm travel to other cities to take classes and discuss issues with other consumer lawyers throughout the country.

As practical application for a consumer, you should ask the lawyer you are interviewing if he/she is a "consumer lawyer who can handle a consumer case?" The lawyer will likely respond as to what kind of consumer protection law umbrella your situation seems to fit. If the lawyer can relay to you the basics of your consumer case, you should know fairly quickly if you are in the correct office.

III. What is "Consumer Law?"

Consumer law is protecting a "consumer" from deceptive acts and practices of a "supplier," using laws enacted by the federal and state legislatures designed to protect the consumer. In other words, it is the laws designed to keep consumers safe from being taken advantage of by a business. It differs from many other areas of the law because it has attorney fees built into it. If a company has been found to have done something wrong, not only to they have to remedy the problem, but they may have to pay for your lawyer.

The law that created the Federal Trade Commission (FTC) Act includes language that prohibits businesses from engaging in "unfair or deceptive acts or practices." Following that, Congress passed an entire "alphabet soup" of laws that were designed to protect consumers. All fifty states, the District of Columbia, Puerto Rico, Guam, and the Virgin Islands followed by putting into place at least one law, with broad application to most consumer transactions, aimed at preventing consumers from being deceived and abused. Most of these laws were created in a ten-year span between the mid-1960s and the mid-1970s. Many of these laws were amended after the original enactment. But, there was a long lull of new law until recently. After the financial crisis of 2008 and the Great Recession, congress passed the Dodd-Frank Consumer Protection and Wall Street Reform Act. This Act created a new agency known as the Consumer Financial Protection Bureau (CFPB). The CFPB has the authority to both enforce the laws that exist, and create rules that support and clarify the existing laws. This is very new, and it is happening in real time. This means that as you read this, the scope of the law is likely changing.

In broad strokes, to be subject to the consumer laws, the transaction at issue must be a consumer transaction between a consumer and a supplier.

IV. What is a Consumer?

That is easy, just about everyone. Everyone reading this book is a consumer. Almost all consumer protection laws are designed to help "natural persons." Remember the law considers corporations and business entities "persons," but those business entities are not reading this book. So, if you have eyeballs, then you are a consumer. And just about everyone who eats, needs transportation, purchases things, applies for credit, or otherwise enters a transaction - is a consumer. So, if you fit the above criteria and purchase something or enter a transaction for your personal use, or for your family, then you probably are a consumer. If you are a corporation or enter into a transaction entirely for commercial use, you probably are not a consumer.

V. What is a "Consumer Transaction?"

Aside from being a natural person, the key aspect to consider when deciding if your issue is a consumer issue is the purpose for which you entered into the transaction. A "consumer transaction" is one where you buy something for yourself, your family, or for household purposes. This includes services as well as products. So, when you buy groceries from the super market, hire a painter for your home, or buy a car, these are consumer transactions. For the most part, it is just a straight forward as it sounds.

It becomes complicated when there is a mixed use. For example, when you use your personal car for work or if you use the same credit card to buy your groceries and for your business. As a general rule, courts look at the primary use. It is often call the "primary use" test. So, if the credit card is mostly used for your daily life and used less often for your business, it likely is a consumer transaction. And, just because you drive your car to work does not necessarily mean it is not subject to the consumer laws.

A car purchase is a good example of a consumer transaction with a bundle of potential consumer issues. It has to do with all aspects of a consumer transaction: (1) a faulty product, (2) misrepresentations in the sale, and (3) misrepresentation in the financing. It is a transaction that entails both a product and a service, all of which have specific laws to protect you.

VI. WHAT IS A "SUPPLIER?"

Suppliers are generally just businesses. Each consumer law has different terms and definitions, but generally, businesses are often referred to in consumer protection statutes as a "merchant" or a "supplier." Examples of what that include are retailers, manufacturers, distributors, dealers, sellers, lessors, assignees, or anyone that, either directing or indirectly, has a part in a consumer transaction with a consumer.

That means that most of the businesses that the average person interacts with on any basis is a supplier. Car dealers, cell companies, credit card companies, banks… the list is practically endless.

VII. WHAT ARE SOME CONSUMER PROTECTION STATUTES?

As mentioned above, a consumer protection statute is a law enacted either by your state legislature or the federal legislature, and is designed to address a particular, abusive business practice. These laws are designed to give consumers the ability to redress an issue or bring a lawsuit that would not otherwise be allowed under traditional law. These laws are different for several important reasons:

1. These laws often have "attorney fee shifting provisions." This means that the consumer's attorney's fees are paid by the offending business if the consumer wins. Under traditional law in most states, a party bringing a lawsuit must pay his/her own attorney fees whether he/she wins or loses. Litigation against a billion-dollar company can be very intensive and expensive. David could never take on Goliath. Attorney fee shifting provisions are designed to level the playing field.

2. Some of statutes allow for "statutory damages." These are damages designed to serve as measuring sticks to allow for damages in consumer cases where the amount of damages is

otherwise hard to quantify. They allow a range of damages a judge could assess against the supplier if the supplier is found to have committed a deceptive practice.

3. Some statutes allow for emotional damages far above what traditional law may allow. The current status of consumer law is to recognize damages for the frustration and embarrassment that a consumer experiences in the process of being wronged by a faceless and uncaring corporation.

4. Some of the statutes allow for punitive damages. These are damages that a jury or judge can award against a deceptive business merely to punish the company for bad behavior. These are damages that may not otherwise be allowed under traditional law. These are damages that often give David an extra weapon against Goliath.

Below is a list of a few of the federal consumer protection statutes:

1. Fair Credit Reporting Act (FRCA) – regulates the collection, dissemination, and use of consumer credit information. This includes credit reports, driving records, employment screening, and most types of background checks.

2. Fair Debt Collection Practices Act (FDCPA) –eliminates deceptive and abusive collection tactics to ensure fairness and common decency as business collect debts.

3. Truth in Lending Act (TILA) – requires clear disclosure of key terms of the lending arrangement and all costs and prohibits the hiding of fees or interest in the fine print.

4. Real Estate Settlement Procedures Act (RESPA) – prohibits kickbacks and requires lenders to provide a good faith estimate of costs and the responsibility of lenders and servicers of loans to respond to questions by homeowners of the status of their accounts.

5. Telephone Consumer Protection Act (TCPA) – limits the use of automatic dialing systems, artificial or prerecorded voice

messages, SMS text messages, and fax machines to consumer land lines and cell phones.

VIII. What is an Example of a Consumer Case?

The main purpose of consumer law is to provide a remedy or relief if you are harmed and the law otherwise doesn't help. How? By something called "fee shifting provisions."

Traditionally, if you are cheated out of $3,000.00 on a car deal you must sue the car dealer for "breach of contract." In most states, you must pay your own attorney's fees. If you pay a lawyer hundreds of dollars an hour to get back your $3000, you'd be throwing good money after bad. It wouldn't make any sense because the case is not economically viable. The entire purpose of the "fee shifting" consumer protection statutes is to allow consumers to bring cases that, under tradition law, could never be economically brought.

So, let's expand on the above example. You go to a big car dealership to buy a car. The salesman tells you the car you are looking at is in "excellent condition" (driven only to church on Sundays by a little, old lady). You look at a Carfax and it says that everything seems to check out, so you buy it. Within a couple of days you: start having problems, find out it has been in wreck or a flood, or you don't get title to the car. You should call a consumer lawyer.

While some clients seek a consumer lawyer because they were saddled with a high interest car loan based upon a deceptive transaction, that is not the most common kind of consumer case. Many times, clients seek a lawyer because their cell phone keeps getting automated calls from a telemarketer, they are constantly harassed by a debt collector, or their credit is misreported by the credit reporting agencies, keeping them from obtaining credit to enable them to happily live their lives. Yet another example is clients that are victims of identity theft and need their credit reports fixed.

Here are some of the primary areas and issues that consumer lawyers handle:

1. **Automobiles** – Anything from the sale, lease, or financing of a vehicle under fraudulent, misleading or deceptive terms. This includes the sale of lemons, and salvaged or wrecked vehicles without proper disclosure.

2. **Repossession** – Any repossession of cars or property done in an unlawful way, either through the use of force or threats or without proper notice.

3. **Credit Reporting** – Includes credit report errors, credit repair scams, privacy invasion, identity theft, and the denial of credit because of improper credit reporting.

4. **Debt Collection** – Debt collectors threatening you or violating the law, wage and bank garnishment, and debt reduction scams.

5. **Mortgage, Real Estate, & Housing** – Any scams or unfair practices related to the sale or financing of a mortgage, home improvement or repairs, foreclosure, landlord and tenant issues, mobile or manufactured homes, and timeshares.

6. **Small Dollar Loans** – Small loan amounts given in exchange for a hold on your paycheck, car title, or tax refund.

7. **Student Loans** – Servicing and collection issues related to federal and private student loans as well as issues related to loans that originated at for-profit institutions.

8. **Telemarketing and Recorded Calls** - Unsolicited faxes, telemarketing calls, or prerecorded or autodialed calls.

9. **Other**– Areas include banking issues, credit cards, deceptive or fraudulent sales practices, financial exploitation, and consumer issues arising out of domestic violence, insurance, utilities, and warranties.

Most consumer lawyers do not charge for a consultation, and because most consumer protection statutes pay for your attorney's fees, many lawyers will take a case on a contingency basis. Consumer laws are complicated and they get confusing in a hurry. So, look for a consumer attorney the minute you feel over your head. It is never too early to seek the advice of a consumer lawyer and there is no reason to have to muddle through this alone.

IX. How do I Find a Consumer Lawyer?

There are not many lawyers who concentrate their practice in consumer law. In theory, that should make it easy to find one! You can ask any lawyer in your city "who knows consumer law?" and he/she will point you to the local expert. But, unfortunately, it usually isn't that easy. Most people start their search on the internet. That is perfectly fine, but there are reasons to use caution. Just as you can't judge a book by its cover, you can't always judge expertise by a flashy webpage. We advise against hiring a distant law firm that does consumer law en masse. These firms rely heavily on internet advertising and not their reputation for clients. Many times, they have little connection to your local legal environment. You want a lawyer who is familiar with the courts, the lawyers, the local defense bar, the juries, and the general temperament of how your jurisdiction reacts to consumer cases like yours. The climate of courts in New York or Los Angeles may be very different in Duluth, Iowa or Kansas City. We suggest starting your search by going to http://www.consumeradvocates.org/find-an-attorney and researching the attorneys in your local area.

X. What do I Ask a Consumer Lawyer?

Obviously, this list is not complete. But it should be helpful for you to get an idea of what kinds of questions to ask:

1. How long have you practiced law in this jurisdiction?
2. How long have you practiced consumer law?
3. Do you have any up front expenses?
4. Am I responsible for any fees up front?
5. Am I responsible for any fees in the end out of my pocket?

6. Am I responsible for any litigation costs up front?
7. Am I responsible for any ligation costs in the end?
8. What are our goals for the litigation?
9. Are we trying to stop the bad behavior or get me money?
10. What amount can I expect?
11. What is the likelihood of this case going to trial?
12. What is the risk to me if I lose?

XI. Conclusion: What Should I Expect from my Consumer Lawyer?

Trust and honesty. I mean that going both directions. Once you find a lawyer who is experienced in consumer law, and that you feel comfortable with, trust him/her. Trust him/her to understand the facts of your case without judging you personally. Don't hide the ugly details from your lawyer. This will only hurt both of you in the end. Your lawyer will give you his/her best, honest assessment of what is going to happen in your case. If you trust his/her judgment, you should trust his/her advice.

We always counsel our clients that a consumer lawsuit is a business transaction to either protect them or do as much "damage control" as we can. It is our belief that you will never punish big business by litigating the principle. You will only punish yourself. We think it is important to stand back, look at the facts as a group of strangers would, while sitting on uncomfortable chairs in a wooden box. Ultimately, that is who will judge your story.

ABOUT THE AUTHOR

Michael Rapp
Partner, Stecklein & Rapp
Chartered
www.giveyourselfcredit.com
Tel: (913) 371-0727

Michael Rapp's practice is focused solely on Consumer Protection cases. Typically, he brings cases against Credit Reporting Agencies, Banks, Credit Card companies and the occasional Debt Collector or shady car lot for doing things that they shouldn't. These cases include both individual and class actions, at State and Federal level.

Michael currently serves as Kansas State Chair for the National Association of Consumer Advocates and as Treasurer for the Solo/Small Section of the Kansas City Metropolitan Bar association. Selected as a Super Lawyers Rising Star for the past 2 years for Kansas and Missouri, Michael frequently presents on the Fair Credit Reporting Act and topics surrounding Consumer Protection Law. Prior to graduating from UMKC School of Law, Michael served his country, was decorated, and honorably discharged from the United States Air Force.

Acknowledgements

The authors would like to thank Angela Miller of Bautista LeRoy LLC for project management and editing, Phil Singleton of KCWebDesigner.com for book production and developing the book's website, and Matt Sain for his research and contributing to the book.

www.ingramcontent.com/pod-product-compliance
Lightning Source LLC
Chambersburg PA
CBHW070247230526
45470CB00002B/502